Start with What

Praise for *Start with What*

"We all endure suffering in life. Stephanie Gray Connors doesn't provide a way to avoid the struggle. Instead, she champions the fact that it doesn't have to negatively define you, can in fact transform you into an even better version of yourself and that in spite of challenging circumstances your best days can indeed remain ahead. With so much negativity and a general sense of victimhood in the world, this book is a counter argument that celebrates the grandeur and possibility of all life… including yours."

–**John O'Leary**
#1 National Bestselling Author of *On Fire* and *In Awe*

"*Start with What* is a moving book. Gray Connors makes a biblical and non-biblical case for why assisted suicide is not the answer for human suffering. As she describes in the book, there is a more loving way. One of my favorite parts about the book is that it is filled with real-life stories that will both challenge and inspire you. I hope you will get a copy of this book, read it, and share it with a friend."

–**Sean McDowell**, Ph.D.
Author, Speaker, Professor

"This excellent volume is an important addition to the critical conversation we must have about the sanctity of life from conception to natural death. While the purpose and focus of Mrs. Gray Connors' fine work is to argue against assisted suicide, it is clear that the significant principles she lays down apply to many of the threats to life that we face in the world today. Through stories that depict real situations that sons and daughters of God have had to grapple with, she elucidates essential principles that guide us away from a culture of death and call for a return to a culture of life. Mrs. Gray Connors shows an uncanny ability to present these dark and difficult scenarios in an uplifting manner, which reinforces the basic point of her work. Life is a precious gift which should be valued in all circumstances. Her treatment of suffering is especially poignant, as it offers the clear truth that even dire suffering does not diminish the ultimate gift that life is. I hope many read this fine book and come to a deeper understanding of the truly sacred character of every human life."

–**Bishop Joseph E. Strickland**

"This is a powerful book about a challenging subject. It will engage you intellectually and also move your heart in a profound way. Well worth the read."

–**Nicole Scheidl**
Executive Director, Canadian Physicians for Life

"Our culture debates the moral questions around suffering through story. Stephanie Gray Connors' new book leverages the persuasive power of narrative to engage your heart and challenge your thinking. I highly recommend it."

–Andy Steiger
President, Apologetics Canada

"For all of human history, we've used stories to teach the most important lessons in life. In this tradition, Gray Connors uses stories to help us grasp that the burden of suffering is to be shared by friends, that all life is to be cherished, and that this is the only truly humane way for us to accompany those crushed by the travails of life."

–Curtis Martin
FOCUS Founder

"Stephanie Gray Connors, in *Start with What: 10 Principles for Thinking about Assisted Suicide*, provides a refreshing contribution to what has become a messy debate. She wastes no time in getting to the point: this is not about assisted suicide itself, or even death, but the fear of meaningless suffering. In her clear and approachable way, she shows the reader how it is reasonable and possible to suffer well, finding strength and joy in the unexpected places of vulnerability and human limitations—thing we already have in plenty. Far from being an idealistic theoretician, Stephanie uses both logic and examples of ordinary persons who have created extraordinary life and love not in spite of, but out of their own suffering. There is much more that could be said about this gem of a book! Stephanie has that rare gift of common sense, which is so uncommon in fact, and this was, although sometimes painful, a most rewarding read."

–Thomas J. Olmsted
Bishop of Phoenix

"It is rare to find serious work on this topic that balances clarity of argument with empathy for those who are suffering. Stephanie has written a profoundly inspiring call to address the whole person in our treatment of debilitating pain. This book will be a great benefit to me in preaching, counselling, and facing end of life decisions with those I love."

–Matthew Menzel
Lead Pastor, Westside Church, Vancouver, BC

"*Start with What* brings much-needed clarity to the divisive topic of assisted suicide. But it does much more than that. It also brings hope. The many stories will leave your heart warmed and motivated to be an instrument of God's love to a world that so desperately needs it."

–Mark Penninga
Executive Director, ARPA Canada

"In *Start with What*, Stephanie Gray Connors not only illuminates your mind with 10 clear ways to combat assisted suicide, she also moves your heart by sharing real life stories, beginning with her own. This book gives us eyes to see that suffering never has the last word, and does not deprive life of beauty and meaning."

–Sister Antoniana Maria Macapagal
Sisters of Life

"Stephanie Gray Connors' compassionate tone and razor sharp intellect makes her one of today's best defenders of pre-born human life. That's why I'm so glad she's taken these gifts and applied to them to a sadly neglected subject in pro-life apologetics: the defense of the elderly, terminally ill, and people with disabilities from assisted suicide and euthanasia. If you want to have a 'roadmap' for approaching this subject then I highly recommend this outstanding work by one of the world's best pro-life advocates."

–Trent Horn
Apologist and author of *Persuasive Pro-life*

"A wise man once said, 'Like apples of gold in settings of silver, so are words spoken in right circumstance.' The circumstances of our day, filled with increasing despair and hopelessness, need such words. My friend Stephanie Gray Connors is uniquely able to present to you truth, kindness, and other forms of gold in these pages. I am confident if you receive what she has prepared for you within, you will find yourself overwhelmed with the wisdom and strength to help yourself and others as despair tempts us to abandon hope. Read eagerly and be filled with the nutrition of wisdom beautifully presented by my gifted friend."

–Todd Wagner
Senior Pastor, Watermark Community Church, Dallas, TX

"Stephanie Gray Connors has long been one of the clearest, sharpest, most winsome pro-life advocates in the world, mostly for her work debating abortion. In this excellent new book, she applies those same gifts to the topic of assisted suicide. The book's strong, pithy principles—such as 'we should alleviate suffering without eliminating the sufferer'—offer ways to reframe the debate, and each principle is illustrated by moving stories. But this is more than a book on ethics or apologetics. It adds profound reflections on the meaning of suffering, and how to find hope and purpose even in the darkest circumstances of life. If every person read this book, the culture of life would flourish. We'd stop assisting suicides, and start celebrating the beauty and significance of all lives, especially those who suffer greatly."

–Brandon Vogt
Founder of ClaritasU and Content Director at Word on Fire Catholic Ministries

"In these pages, Stephanie Gray Connors grips the heart, the soul and the mind. This is not a sterile treatise on bioethics, but a heartfelt and rational defense of life in the fullest sense, in a world increasingly seduced by the easy, false and deadly answers buried in terms such as Dying with Dignity and MAiD. This book is worth reading, sharing, and acting upon."

–**Dr. Pascal Bastien**, MD FRCPC
Specialist in General Internal Medicine, Executive, Toronto Catholic Doctors' Guild

"Stephanie Gray Connors' newest book, *Start with What*, is an excellent, life-affirming book on the subject of assisted suicide. She covers the topic well from a Biblical, emotional, practical, and medical perspective. Her real-life stories are very moving and also illustrate her 10 principles so well. This book illustrates the value of the Christian worldview, especially its view of people made in God's image and therefore worth preserving from conception to the grave. I highly recommend it."

–**Bobby Parks**
Executive Director, Christian Medical Ministry of Alabama

"I have always admired Stephanie's ability to make the case for the unborn child in an equally persuasive and kind manner. Her many conferences on the issue are a great example of how productive and uncommon this approach is. In *Start With What: 10 Principles for Thinking about Assisted Suicide*, Stephanie really reaches the peak of her style. She not only fully accomplishes her goal of making 'a winsome and persuasive pro-life case on assisted suicide to those who do not share our worldview,' but takes the conversation to a fascinating and unexpected level: to an honest discussion of why we suffer, why we consider suicide a tragedy and how we can find a sensible common ground when we agree upon the evidence: both the inevitability and the hidden value of suffering. The book is a rich, enjoyable and compelling balance of life examples, commonsensical arguments and a broad mix of ideas, both religious and not. Thus, Stephanie's book runs like a novel, teaches like a catechism, and prepares like a manual. It is highly recommended for everyone I can think of. Because everyone I can think of knows that life includes suffering, that we are going to die, and that we all want to make the best of the time we have been given on this earth."

–**Alejandro Bermudez**
Executive Director, CNA/ACI Group

"*Start with What* teaches us how to respond with charity and truth to the increasing advocacy for and acceptance of assisted suicide. Stephanie Gray Connors provides eternal hope and purpose to people in the midst of intense suffering when the world wants to focus on despair and aid and hasten death."

–**Jim Graham**
President and Executive Director of Texas Right to Life

"Stephanie Gray Connors is an articulate, passionate, and wholly committed advocate for the dignity of life. Since her teenage years, Stephanie has shared her pro-life/pro-family message, passionately advocating for a person's right to life regardless of ability, circumstance, or age. Stephanie's message is one of gentleness, compassion, and love—a message of never giving up hope and why caring for our most vulnerable is one of our Lord's greatest gifts."
                                                              –Bobby Schindler
                                                Terri Schiavo Life & Hope Network

"Stephanie Gray Connors' book *Start with What* is a poignantly written work that brings tremendous clarity to an issue that is often shrouded in euphemisms and misunderstandings. Stephanie has done a great service in illuminating the principles that underlie the prohibition to take the lives of others, and she does so through her gift of story-telling. The result is a masterful work that not only brings to this issue crystal clarity, but also inspires all of us to understand the great and perplexing question of human suffering. I give her five stars for this illuminating work!"
                                                              –Natalie Sonnen
                  Executive Director of LifeCanada, Author of LifeCanada's *Dying Healed* Program

"I enjoyed reading the new book by Stephanie Gray Connors–*Start with What: 10 Principles for Thinking about Assisted Suicide*. Gray Connors deals with the issues of assisted suicide by sharing inspirational stories of people who have overcome great human challenges. She doesn't lessen the reality of the human challenges but rather she sheds a new light on those challenges. Gray Connors shares a faith-filled perspective but not in an imposing manner. Her writing style and stories keep you wanting to read more, they keep you interested in the outcome and she interconnects one story and its outcome to the next. In my more than 20 years of experience with issues concerning death and dying and after speaking with many people who were dealing with difficult human realities, I have learned that people who have hope, people who have significant community, people who feel a sense of purpose, aren't seeking death by suicide, assisted suicide or euthanasia. Gray Connors helps us find that hope, that sense of purpose, and inspires you to be significant community to others. When killing becomes a reality in society it only begets more killing. It leads to more problems that are answered by killing. This is a book that inspires society to care for people in their time of need and helps us to understand outcomes of caring for people rather than killing. You need to read this book. It's truly an inspiration."
                                                           –Alex Schadenberg
                                    Executive Director, Euthanasia Prevention Coalition

"In her eloquent, thoughtful and deeply personal way, Stephanie weaves together clear-cut logic and gipping stories to present not only a compelling case against assisted suicide, but also a case for the alternatives we should instead be seeking. Grab a journal (and maybe a box of tissues too) because you will be taken by the accounts of heroic souls who made their experience of profound hardship a pathway for spreading hope, as well as those who were elevated from the brink of despair through connection, creativity and beauty. This book will cause you to consider what makes a society truly civil, and what makes a decision truly compassionate. No doubt, you will be inspired to find meaning in your own—and others'—circumstances, no matter how challenging."

–Cristina Barba Whalen
CEO & Founder, The Culture Project

"I highly recommend this thoughtful and inspiring book to all. Through multiple storytelling, the author leads the reader to seriously consider and think about these real issues of suffering, thoughts of suicide, and assisted suicide. The book helps to find better ways for those suffering now, and shows all of us ways to help these individuals. The scope of suffering, the importance of having a meaningful purpose, and the power of relationships, love, and God are examined and demonstrated in this book. I pray that I can put into practice what this book teaches."

–Dr. Jim Lane
President, Vancouver Catholic Physicians Guild

"Stephanie Gray Connors' book is a cry of the heart that challenges each of us to let suffering unleash love, creativity, and compassion. It's a call to recognize the dignity and worth of life at every stage, especially when a person is in their darkest moments of pain and suffering. Your mind will be opened by Stephanie's skill and wisdom in presenting the case against assisted suicide, and your heart will be moved by the stories of people who allow love to have the last word in the face of the universal human experience of pain and suffering."

–Michael Hall
Senior Content Development Specialist, Catholic Christian Outreach Canada

"As a friend, mentor, and role-model, Stephanie never fails to convince me (unknowingly) that she was sent by God for a time such as this. I salute her with all my heart, and cannot recommend her latest book to you enough. She cracks open a difficult conversation that is at our very doorsteps, one we need to be informed about. Stephanie, through the art of story-telling, makes that process enjoyable."

–Katie Ascough
Journalist and founder of *calledtomore.org*

"'Dying with dignity'? Stephanie Gray Connors fuses common sense with profound insights derived from faith in the living God to argue what that should mean. Hers is the most engaging presentation for a general readership I've seen. The damaging effects of euthanasia on health care professionals, the degradation arising from pressure on the elderly to 'get out of the way,' and how we all lose once we've forgotten how to find meaning in suffering, are all exposed. And the stories—riveting and rousing—are alone worth the price of the book."

–**Peter Galadza**
Professor Emeritus, Sheptytsky Institute of Eastern Christian Studies, University of St. Michael's College in the University of Toronto

"This book is unlike any other book on assisted suicide. It exposes, in a compelling way, the illusion of complete individual autonomy—the 'enlightened dream' that never comes true. But Stephanie Gray Connors goes beyond the philosophical argument and describes in her uniquely eloquent and approachable style, the human depth of life, suffering and death: How do we experience meaning, flourish, create human connection and relationship, and what has this all to do with the 'art of dying well'? With euthanasia and assisted suicide laws on the rise, from New Zealand to Canada, from Belgium to Colombia, this book puts words to the mysterious beauty of human life that persists even in suffering. This is a must read for anyone who wants to go beyond populist headlines that suggest that assisted suicide is necessary for a humane society."

–**Sophia Kuby**
Director of Strategic Relations & Training, ADF International

"This is a book which packs a lot of stories, a lot of emotion and a lot of good sense. Proponents of assisted suicide have stolen a march in the campaign to bring about legislative change, in various jurisdictions around the world, so often relying on the power of story. This book goes much deeper than euthanasia supporters dare go, in order to give us profound encounters with people who demonstrate how the life-embracing attitude is the one which genuinely reflects the dignity of every human life. You may weep with sadness and joy, but this book does much more than just present the emotional arguments against assisted suicide. It effectively deals with all the important areas of ethical consideration and decision-making that confront us at the end of life."

–**John Deighan**
CEO, Society for the Protection of Unborn Children (SPUC) Scotland

"*Start with What* offers a unique perspective on an issue that is emotionally charged, highly politicized, and largely misunderstood. This book is not an academic treatise against assisted suicide. Instead, it challenges the practice by employing simple but profound stories of real people who struggled against illness and pain, yet found purpose in their suffering. The book is a valuable resource for all, but perhaps mostly for those who—diagnosed with a serious, even terminal, condition—are contemplating ending their lives. It offers clear, logical reasons for people not to kill themselves."

–Joe Zalot, Ph.D.
National Catholic Bioethics Center

"What do we do with the problem of suffering? This perennial question is addressed with wisdom and brilliance by Stephanie, who has dedicated her life to helping others see the value of every single life, no matter their struggles. A must-read for anyone who hopes to make our world better and more loving."

–Lila Rose
Founder and President of Live Action, Author of *Fighting for Life*

"This is an amazing piece of work. Profound, uplifting, insightful, and easy to read. This book is essential reading for anyone that is, or will be, dealing with end of life issues, depression, or any type of pain or suffering. I wish I would have had it a few years ago when dealing with my parents' and other family members' end of life issues."

–Don Hood
President of Worldviews, Calling & Culture Inc.

Start with What

10 Principles for Thinking about Assisted Suicide

Stephanie Gray Connors

Copyright © 2020 by Stephanie Gray Connors

All rights reserved. No part of this publication may be reproduced, distributed, or transmitted in any form or by any means, including photocopying, recording, or other electronic or mechanical methods, without the prior written permission of the author, except in the case of brief quotations embodied in critical reviews and certain other noncommercial uses permitted by copyright law.

Cover design by *Just Serviam*.

Wongeese Publishing
Florida

Start with What: 10 Principles for Thinking about Assisted Suicide / Stephanie Gray Connors—1st ed.

ISBN: 978-1-7364544-0-4

Dedication

To my beloved husband Joe—"God blessed the broken road that led me straight to you."[1]

And to our precious child Laetificat Judah—LaeLae, you left my womb too early, but you will remain in our hearts forever.

Contents

Preface xvii

Introduction xix

1 Start by Asking What 1

2 If Humans are Equal, We all Ought to Get Suicide Prevention 11

3 Suffering Unleashes Love 24

4 We Can Alleviate Suffering without Eliminating Sufferers 38

5 Human Dignity is Unconditional 56

6 Human Flourishing Occurs in a Context of Connection 64

7 We Ought to Celebrate Being 71

8 Some of the Best Things in Life Come When We Release Control 79

9 Not all Choices are Equal, but They Create a Ripple Effect Either Way . 90

10 Beauty and Creativity are Transformative 96

Epilogue 107

About the Author 119

Acknowledgments 121

Endnotes 122

Preface

Is this book written for you?

If you're human, if you've suffered, and if you will one day die, then the answer is yes.

When I first sat down to write this book, I thought very intentionally about my audience. Initially, the criteria was narrower than the above. I speak often to Christian audiences, of various denominations, and I wanted to write largely to that demographic. And yet, I also wanted to equip fellow Christians to make a winsome and persuasive pro-life case on assisted suicide to those who do not share our worldview. What of those who embrace a different religion? Or no religion? Perhaps that's you.

Thinking of these other audiences, one of my friends, who read a draft of this book, suggested I make two versions—one with religious appeals and one without. She felt that the non-sectarian arguments within were important enough to be heard by non-Christians and didn't want a book with religious references to be overlooked by that audience.

This prompted me to think about the many books a person reads in a lifetime. How often are we inspired, educated, or activated by a book whose author, if we dug deep enough, does not agree with every single thing we believe? Now I realize in the case of my book, if you do not share my worldview, you won't have to dig too deep; I make some overt religious references. And yet, I actually think this can be helpful: How often do those who do not believe in God wonder, quite incredulously, how Christians reconcile the notion of a good God with a world of great suffering? At the very least, I hope this book will satisfy some of that curiosity.

A book, like a movie, is made up of different parts—one person can be captivated by a particular scene that his friend is not. Well beyond worldviews, our personalities, life experience, education, and so forth, are all factors which influence which messages resonate and which do not. And so, in what follows I offer a broad mix of ideas—both sectarian *and* non-sectarian.

It is my hope that there is at least something within that activates the mind and stirs the heart. After all, although we who read this are most certainly alive, we will all most certainly die. And until then, at various points, we will all most certainly suffer. In light of that reality, this book seeks to propose a way of thinking that will help us, and our loved ones, flourish on our journeys.

~Stephanie Gray Connors
November 2020

Introduction

It happened back in 2015 but I remember it like it was yesterday.

It was late May and it had been sunny and warm. It was my favorite time of day: "Golden Sunlight," as one of my photographer-friends refers to it, the best natural lighting for taking pictures outdoors. I was in my favorite city—Vancouver—which is also my birthplace and has been my home at various points in adulthood. Vancouver is situated along the coast of the province in which the license plates say "***Beautiful*** British Columbia" for a reason. I was at one of the most stunning parts of the city, the peninsula on which rests my alma mater, The University of British Columbia. There are many lookouts for your eyes to feast on the breathtaking scene of vast ocean becoming one with the ever-changing sky. The sun was setting and it was simply gorgeous out. But as I sat in the car with my fiancé, the darkest season of my life was about to begin.

Our engagement had just come to an end, and so did, it felt like, the dream of a lifetime. A purchased dress would remain unworn. A ring finger would no longer display glittering diamonds that indicated the wearer was *chosen*. But most significant of all, a heart that had finally fallen in love would now endure a death-like loss. As I left his car to sit in mine, I remember beginning to cry. Wail is more like it. From the depths of my being the suffering—the anguish—was so profound that I sounded like an animal caught in a trap. I felt utterly crushed. Decimated. Hopeless.

I called my sister and my cousin and I remember exactly what I said to them:

"I don't want to live. I want to die."

My cousin picked me up and my sister drove to meet us. My car was left behind, and that, in a sense, was a metaphor for what I was experiencing—the power of mobility trapped in a stationary state. Heaviness. Abandonment. But the response of my family members, the literal picking up, would also act as a metaphor for how I was to eventually find healing—to be lifted, carried, connected, and surrounded.

Suffering takes all forms. For the person who wants to be married, it appears as a broken heart or an unfulfilled desire for romantic relationship. For the person who wants children, it presents as an empty womb or empty arms. For the person who wants to walk, it presents as paralysis, broken legs, or, even, no legs. For the person who wants to see, it presents as blindness. For the person who wants a job, it presents as unemployment and mounting debt. For the person who wants to feel comfort or even just "normal," it presents as chronic pain. This list could go on.

Each experience is so different and yet there is a common thread to all: A wish that is not, and maybe cannot be, fulfilled. A deep longing which is temporarily, or even permanently, going to be unmet.

And the clash of what one wants and what one has creates the explosive force that we call suffering.

Suffering is part of the human experience. It cannot be avoided. But it can be shared. And it is when we share it, when we enter into it, when we wrestle and do battle with it, when we respond to it with creativity, it is then that we begin to discover the power of suffering not just in the crushing but also in the re-building, the drawing-in, and the uniting.

This makes me think of a song by *Hillsong Worship*: "In the crushing, in the pressing, you are making new wine."[2]

Over the two decades of my public speaking and writing career, I have continually declared that we should alleviate suffering without eliminating the sufferer. As time passes, I am more convinced than ever of the truthfulness of that statement—not simply that we should do this, but that we actually ***can*** successfully do it. But note this important observation: to alleviate is not to eliminate. I do not think we can entirely eliminate suffering from the profoundly broken and imperfect world we live in. We can certainly try, but if we fail we must remember that there is still hope—and that the hope lies in ***alleviating*** suffering; it lies in bringing beauty from ashes.

The importance of alleviating suffering without eliminating sufferers is so needed in a world where suicide is on the rise, where there is a segment of the population whose suffering is so overwhelming that death seems better than life.

When I was a child, I remember being taught at school about suicide. I remember being told that suicidal ideation was one secret we shouldn't keep—that if a friend expressed that she (or he) was thinking about killing herself, that we should get help. I was taught that we needed to make sure our friends were safe, cared for, and protected from self-harm.

A quick Google search of "I'm suicidal" provides results leading people to help with suicide prevention. Advertisements with messages of support for people in such distress are in bathrooms, schools, and, as I've noticed in my travels, even in airports.

So many have been personally touched by suicide. A couple decades ago, the dad of one of my friends committed suicide. About 10 years ago, a friend I knew from my university days committed suicide. And as I write this, one of my friends' uncles committed suicide. When suicide happens, people grieve. When famous people die by suicide, whether it be Robin Williams, Kate Spade, or Anthony Bourdain (to name a few), the world responds with sorrow. When the news reports on suicide, whether with headlines like "Why US Suicide Rate is on the Rise" from the *BBC*[3] or "Suicide Rates Sharply Increase Among Girls" from *Forbes*,[4] suicide is presented as a bad—not a good—thing. Typically, at the bottom of news stories about suicide, there is a message to readers to seek help if they are suicidal.

And yet, there's an interesting dichotomy occurring: While society generally decries suicide, there is an increasing acceptance of it when the word "assisted" is placed in front.

Assisted suicide (and its close cousin euthanasia) are being legalized, or at the very least debate about their legalization is occurring, in various parts of the world. Whether someone solicits another to provide a life-ending substance that he administers himself, or whether he asks another to administer a life-ending substance for him, the end result is the same: Someone dies because he expressed a wish to, and another party assists him in some way in achieving his stated goal. Whereas suicide happens in isolation, assisted suicide involves other-party participation.

And that leads to the topic of this book. Should suicide ever be assisted? When one no longer wishes to live, and asks another to help him end his life, what is the right response?

This book provides an answer to that. In short, it makes the case that **suicide should never be assisted**. The simple premise is this: If suicide is wrong and if homicide is wrong, then uniting the two in a situation where you have a type of suicide/homicide does not make them right; instead, the combination is just as wrong. That should be obvious, but because for many it is not, this book relies on the vehicle of storytelling to provide the narrative on the other side of the argument that is typically not heard.

Why stories? Stories are a powerful means through which principles are demonstrated. That's why major world religions from Judaism to Christianity, from Islam to Sikhism, from Hinduism to Buddhism, make stories a core part of their teachings.[5] In some sense it's as though learning-by-storytelling is built into our nature, starting with young children who delight in having stories read to them. This fascination with stories never really leaves us, and can be seen in adults' interest in movies, novels, magazines, and even social media—all being avenues through which stories are told.

Stories captivate the imagination and engage the mind. They also are a way of sharing one's subjective experience. And that is where storytelling to defend a position on an issue can be tricky. Whenever you rely on a story to make a point there is a risk that someone who holds an alternate view will dismiss the story as a subjective experience, and argue for an alternative point using a different story. The idea being that one subjective experience can cancel out the other, leaving both parties no further down the road in bolstering one's position.

But sharing stories can be more than re-telling a subjective experience. When objective principles are identified, they are more readily embraced when inserted *into* a story. In this case, the story does not become the argument. The story is merely the vehicle through which the argument is made clear. It becomes the means to help the mind comprehend the lesson.

Consider, for example, *Aesop's Fables*. In the story about the wind and the sun the point is this: "Gentleness and kind persuasion win where force and bluster fail."[6] Then, a story is built around that; namely, a fable about the wind and the sun debating amongst themselves about who can convince a man walking down the road to remove his coat. The wind believes blowing hard will do so, but rather than blowing the coat off, it results in the man holding his coat close. The sun, however, quietly, calmly, and gradually comes out from behind the clouds and as its warm temperatures heat up the environment, the man removes his coat.

When it comes to assisted suicide, this book suggests 10 principles that should guide peoples' thinking on the topic. It then draws on various stories to make those points abundantly clear and easily embraced. If followed, these guideposts will lead to human flourishing.

1
Start by Asking What

Matt Hampson and Dan James had many things in common: they were close in age, being born within a year of each other. They hailed from England. They were promising rugby players. When the men were in their early twenties, they were in separate scrummage accidents. They became paralyzed.

As a result of this, they both suffered profoundly. Today, Matt has turned that suffering into a source of meaning. He started the Matt Hampson Foundation to help people who have been catastrophically hurt in sporting accidents. Through his foundation, Matt was instrumental in developing the "Get Busy Living Centre" where people with injuries come to get rehabilitation, encouragement, and community. He is a mentor, motivational speaker, writer, and rugby coach.[7] He does all of this while using a wheelchair and a ventilator.

When Matt gave a *TEDxLeicester Talk* he concluded it by saying: "We can get busy living, or get busy dying. And I've decided to get busy living."[8]

Matt's focus on life, on the positive contribution he can make, aligns with this Scriptural advice from Philippians 4:8: "…whatever is true, whatever is honorable, whatever is just, whatever is pure, whatever is lovely, whatever is gracious, if there is anything worthy of praise, think about these things."[9]

While Matt got busy living, tragically Dan got busy dying. After his injuries, Dan was so overwhelmed that he attempted suicide multiple times.[10] This culminated in him travelling to Switzerland in 2008 where, at the age of 23, he went to a clinic and was provided a lethal drink that he consumed.[11]

There is no denying that a life of paralysis is a cross of tremendous weight to bear.[12] If you are a quadriplegic, you cannot feed yourself, turn yourself, or toilet yourself. If you are dependent on a ventilator, you cannot even breathe on your own. Secondary complications from paralysis can include bladder and bowel issues, deep vein thrombosis, sepsis, pressure sores, spasticity, and more.[13] These realities point to suffering that is physical, as well as one that is emotional, since it leads to losing independence as one knew it, relying on others for deeply personal and private care that can feel uncomfortable surrendering to.

If it is fair to say both Dan and Matt suffer(ed) greatly in their paralyzed states, what explains the different responses of these men who had shared experiences? I believe the answer lies in the insight of psychiatrist and Holocaust-survivor Dr. Viktor Frankl, who not only endured profound personal suffering, but who had experience guiding those who suffered as well. In a recorded interview, Dr. Frankl remarked that "despair is suffering without meaning."[14] He captured the concept with the following mathematical equation:

$$D = S - M$$

His point is that S (suffering) is a reality of the human experience. But whether someone despairs (D) in light of suffering is entirely dependent on whether they find meaning (M). To the extent that they find meaning in their suffering, despair goes down. But if they find no meaning in their suffering, despair goes up. And it's despair that can lead to suicide.[15]

Finding meaning is possible even when the situation is bleak. Dr. Frankl cites a teenager in Texas who became a quadriplegic, yet she did not despair as others in her situation (like Dan) have. What set this young woman apart was not her experience of suffering but her response to it: She spent her days reading newspapers and watching television for an important purpose—whenever there was a story about someone experiencing difficult and challenging times, she would have a stick placed in her mouth so she could use it to press keys to type out letters of encouragement, consolation, and hope to the people she read about.[16] She turned her experience of suffering into a springboard to reach out to others; it enabled her to have empathy and share hope. In short, she found meaning.

Or take another person with quadriplegia, a young man who became paralyzed at 17 years old. Dr. Frankl received a letter from him: *"I broke my neck but it did not break me."*[17] Why, like the aforementioned young woman, did this man not despair? Because he found meaning in his situation: He decided to become a psychologist, realizing that what he experienced would help him connect with, and aid, patients.

When speaking of people like these two young adults, Dr. Frankl said, *"They can mold… their predicament into an accomplishment on the human level; they can turn their tragedies into a personal triumph. But they must know for what—what should I do with it?"*[18]

The key word there is "what." Whereas bestselling author Simon Sinek teaches people to *Start with Why*,[19] one could say that suffering can teach people to *Start with What*. It teaches people to ask, "What can I do in light of this? What good can I draw from it?" Of course, suffering people are tempted to start with why, asking questions like, "Why did this happen to me?" and "Why must I go through this?" In fact, in his *TEDx Talk*, Matt spoke about going through the stage of asking himself "the whys." But when terribly profound suffering happens to one and not others, "Why me?" is not easily answered. When news headlines tell us about people kidnapped and tortured, about children turned into sex slaves, about people victimized by genocide, the question "Why?" leaves us feeling empty-handed. Sure, we might say it's because we live in an imperfect world, because evil exists, or because life isn't fair, but does that satisfy?

The inability to adequately explain or be satisfied by "Why?" can leave us feeling more frustrated, adding an additional suffering to the pre-existing suffering. But when we ask, "***What***? ***What*** can I do now? ***What*** can I do because of this? ***What*** good can I draw from it?" then we get answers. Then we get empowerment. Then we get transformation. Making our "what" something positive that comes in direct response to a suffering that is negative does not suddenly transform the negative into something that is good in and of itself. It does not make a case ***for suffering***. It accepts that there is an element of mystery to suffering. Instead, what it does do is make a case ***for bringing good out of suffering***.

It is worth emphasizing that when good comes out of suffering, that good does not make the original suffering good. For example, imagine a woman is raped, gets pregnant, and the resulting child grows up to find the cure for cancer. It is an incredible good that an unrepeatable and irreplaceable individual accomplished such a wonderful thing. But that good fruit does not make the original rape (and the untold suffering the mother experienced) a good thing. The end does not justify the means, and so if we had a magical power to go back in history and prevent the rape from happening, we should do that. We could never justify committing evil (rape) just to bring about a good (conceive a human who will discover the cure for cancer). However, no such ability to undo the past exists. We cannot undo the evil and suffering that occurred. Since we are only left with the present and the future, we can choose to do good ***in response to*** bad things from the past.

And so, when anyone in a situation of profound suffering is tempted to ask "Why?" we should lead them to this insight:

> Maybe you're starting with the wrong question. Maybe the question shouldn't be 'Why?' Maybe the question should be 'What?' Maybe the question should be, 'What am I going to do about this?' Maybe the question should be, 'What marvelous, amazing, wonderful thing am I going to create in response to this terrible, horrific, awful thing?' Maybe the question shouldn't be so much about the reason for the past ('Why did that happen?') as it should be about a response for the future ('What's next?').

"What now?" or "What good can I do in light of this?" is a question Patrick John Hughes asked himself. In March 1988, when his son Patrick Henry was born, the exciting news of "It's a boy!" was met with a series of negative news: That boy had no eyes. He had scoliosis. He had an inability to straighten his arms and legs, which would mean life in a wheelchair. Patrick John and his wife experienced understandable suffering that accompanies an unwell child and dashed dreams. Active sports like baseball would not be a part of their father-son relationship. So many things Patrick Henry would never do. Patrick John and his wife naturally asked themselves why,[20] but eventually they shifted to what—what can we do in response to this unexpected reality? In a short matter of time, it became obvious that Patrick Henry was a musical prodigy. At only 9 months old he began playing piano and today, having never seen a note, is an accomplished pianist, singer, and trumpet player.

Patrick John and Patrick Henry are an inspiring father-son duo. When Patrick Henry got the opportunity to play trumpet in the University of Louisville Marching Band, it was his father who pushed him in his wheelchair so he could "march" along. When Patrick Henry attended university, it was his father who accompanied him to classes.[21] When Patrick wrote a book, it was his father who co-authored it with him.[22]

There is much Patrick Henry cannot do, and that can be cause for suffering. But there is much he **can** do, and that is where he stays focused.

Lord of the Rings even "starts with what." In the first film, Frodo says to the wise wizard Gandalf, "I wish the Ring had never come to me. I wish none of this had happened." And Gandalf replies, "So do all who live to see such times, but that is not for them to decide. All we have to decide is **what** [emphasis added] to do with the time that is given to us."[23]

"What now?" or "What good can I do in light of this?" is a question Michael Morton asked himself. There aren't words to fully capture the cruel suffering Michael endured for over two decades. It all began in 1986, when his beloved wife Christine was brutally murdered. As if that weren't bad enough, their 3-year-old son was home when the murder occurred. It gets even worse. Within weeks, Michael was arrested for murdering his wife and sentenced to life in prison—except he did not commit the crime. For almost 25 long, agonizing, brutal years (or, as Michael puts it, 8,980 days), Michael was robbed of his freedom through unjust incarceration.[24]

Not only did he have to grieve the loss of his wife in a prison cell, not only was he ripped away from raising his son, not only did he have a destroyed reputation, but he was forced to live with some of the worst criminals (fearing beatings, rapes, and even murder that some prisoners inflicted on their fellow inmates). Michael spent time doing back-breaking labor under blazing Texas heat in fields amidst fire ants, mosquitos, snakes, and alligators. He endured freezing temperatures indoors during winter and overwhelmingly hot temperatures indoors during summer.

So much suffering, for so long. Why did such misery happen to Michael? Why him? How far does answering those questions get us? But *what* could he do about it? There we have answers; in fact, Michael chose a series of positive "whats" in response: He spent time in the prison library, studying case law and how appeals worked; he participated in a prison book club; he completed his college education from jail, majoring in psychology; he then pursued graduate studies from a different prison; he jogged and lifted weights; he journaled his experiences; he wrote arguments for his innocence as well as composed short stories (some of which were published in small magazines).[25]

When his case was eventually taken on by The Innocence Project,[26] an organization that works to exonerate the wrongly convicted, their brilliant efforts and DNA-testing technology identified the actual murderer and freed Michael in 2011.

Even though his suffering of unjust imprisonment was lifted, Michael continued with a focus on "what" he could do as a result of what he had faced. He became a public speaker before retiring. He pursued a case against prosecutor Ken Anderson for how he mishandled Michael's trial. He did this, not out of revenge but out of justice. Michael wrote in his book,

> Even though I would have liked nothing better than to simply go home and begin rebuilding what was left of my life, I couldn't

walk away from my case or the glaring problems it exposed. If making a difference meant spending more time in courtrooms, if it meant speaking to state lawmakers—if it meant becoming more of a public person than I had ever intended to be—I had an obligation to do it…There were people just like me still in prison. If the system didn't change, there would be more in the future.[27]

A very powerful "what" indeed.

"What now?" or "What good can I do in light of this?" is a question my friend Lisa asked herself. Sixteen years ago, when Lisa was in her late teens she found herself on a psychiatric ward, confined there for a month due to psychosis. She was to eventually be diagnosed with Bipolar Disorder Type II. Her reality of mental illness has led to all kinds of suffering, including suicidal ideation, depression, and manic episodes. And yet, the word Lisa lives by is **resilience**. She has chosen to turn her deeply personal mental health struggles into a means to help and inspire others. She regularly writes a column for a newspaper, is working on her memoir, hosts a podcast, and is a public speaker on mental health. More than that, in further asking herself "What can I do in light of this?" Lisa has joined various groups designed to teach wellness, including drawing on the insights of cognitive behavioral therapy. Not only has she been a student of these programs, but now she is a mentor in them, helping others find wellness. Her days are filled with God, work, friendship, family, connection, meeting new people, music, writing,[28] poetry, walks, and purpose. Living with the challenges of bipolar disorder is not easy—it's certainly overwhelming at times; and yet, as a result of it, she has become intentional about what is needed to make her thrive in light of that reality. In identifying that, she then works to help others do the same.

"What now?" or "What good can I do in light of this?" is something my friends Peter and Anne[29] asked themselves. Anne lived for decades struggling with debilitating environmental allergies and Parkinson's disease. Her allergies were so severe she had to wear an industrial gas mask. Their home had to be isolated, meaning their windows remained closed—year round. As her condition worsened, trips away, something Peter enjoyed so much, could no longer be accomplished. After more than 10 years of these challenges, Anne was diagnosed with Parkinson's, which she endured for 17 years. As her ailments worsened, she focused on *what* she could do nonetheless. And her whats became sewing for her grandchildren, creating memory albums, cooking at home, and praying for others. She enjoyed passing time with crossword puzzles, Sudoku, and chess. And of course, the gift of time was also passed with the gift of family—the presence of her husband and visits from her children and grandchildren. Life went on, but life went on close to home. That slower-pace, house-bound life of hers also became his. One day, in the spring of 2017, Peter and Anne would dance together, not at a fancy hotel ballroom, but in the simplicity of their living room where home was simply "being with"—home was where the other was. Tragically, three days later, Anne would unexpectedly pass away, creating a void for Peter that words cannot express.

Besides the obvious emptiness in his heart, there was a whole new emptiness in his daily life, and Peter suddenly found himself with a wealth of time. And so, he asked himself *what* all the time and ability to be away from home now enabled him to do. Answering that has led to a wealth of experiences involving creativity, contribution, and connection. Peter wrote me,

> I had come to know other people who were shut-ins in wheelchairs with chronic debilitating illnesses and decided that I would start visiting them regularly at home or hospital. It quickly became evident how lonely these people are (as visitors are very sparse and far in between) and are starved for conversation. Sometimes I am the only regular visitor. The visits are about 'being with, listening to and talking to.' In reality we are ministering to one another and new friendships are formed.

He also spent a year teaching a religion class to 9-year-olds. And he regularly ministers to homeless women who are street workers. His decision, in his pain and loneliness, to help others in their need, reminds me of the words of Dr. Frankl: ***"The more one forgets himself—by giving himself to a cause to serve or another person to love—the more human he is."***[30]

Peter's flourishing amidst suffering continues: He co-started and participates in a men's book club and joined a Bible study. He made a serious return to the piano with weekly lessons and daily practice of at least two hours. He also encouraged his teacher to organize social gatherings with mini recitals of amateur adult pianists, telling me, "I believe that there are many people out there who play, that the sharing of good music has great transcendental and therapeutic value and that such informal events should be encouraged."

Those words became very real to him in a recent encounter he had: Two Jehovah Witness ladies knocked on his door while he was practicing piano. He decided to invite them in and play Beethoven's *Fur Elise* for them. They had never heard it before and were quite moved; in fact, one of them started to cry.

He wrote me,

> I feel that the music, played from the heart, took them aback, yet somehow spoke to them on a level transcending their norm, especially to the one who shed tears. The experience has further consolidated the awareness of my role in this life: I am just a steward and a servant making use of my limited talents to pass on some ineffable thing far greater, a discernment in no way diminished after becoming a retired widower.

The death of one's soulmate. Chronic physical illness. Mental illness. Unjust imprisonment. Birth defects. Paralysis. These are significant sufferings. People can, and do, respond to each in a negative way. But the above stories are proof that people can, and do, respond in a positive way too. The determining factor is in "starting with what," in the search for meaning, in the search for ***what*** good can come from suffering.

When someone no longer wishes to live and desires assisted suicide, those around them should assist—not with suicide—but with helping the person discover their "what?"

Perhaps their what is to empathize with another suffering soul, to become a writer, to be a listener, to teach people how to slow down and enter into the present moment, to become an advocate for finding a cure for a disease, to leave a lesson for loved ones or perhaps even strangers working in a hospital of what really matters in life, of how to surrender, of how to release control. Their "what" could simply be to teach others, by their need and total dependence, the life-changing power of vulnerability and love.

The "whats" of the people featured in this chapter are proof that it is possible to not merely survive amidst suffering but to actually thrive, to discover a whole new world of opportunity, beauty, creativity, joy, and relationship—even amidst the pain, and, perhaps, because of it. But typically we don't discover this on our own. Typically we need to be *assisted*. So, rather than assisted suicide, we should "start with what" and seek out assisted searches for meaning.

2

If Humans are Equal, We all Ought to Get Suicide Prevention

On March 11, 2005, two men would meet and be forever changed. Kevin Berthia and Kevin Briggs had a chance encounter at one of San Francisco's top tourist attractions: The Golden Gate Bridge. Berthia had never been before whereas Briggs was a regular there. Neither, however, were tourists themselves. Separated by age, work, and life experience, they were brought together by one thing: Suicide.

Briggs was a California Highway Patrol officer on duty at the bridge that day. Berthia showed up to jump off of it. Since childhood, Berthia had struggled with severe depression. He had a baby who was born premature and because she had to spend eight weeks in the hospital, he was faced with a $200,000+ medical bill Berthia could not afford. Things were so desperate financially he couldn't even pay for a Christmas present for his beloved daughter.[31] He was overwhelmed, and thought the way out was death.

Unaware of those details, Briggs, responded to a call about a possible suicide attempt. Berthia had jumped over the railing and was teetering on the ledge. A conversation began, and Briggs mostly listened as

Berthia spoke for an hour and a half about all that was overwhelming him.[32]

More than 200 people are alive today because of Briggs' intervention on the bridge.[33] Thankfully Berthia is one of them. Now, more than a decade since that incident, Berthia is a father to three children, a suicide prevention advocate, and has been a presenter at *TEDx*.

Briggs is rightly celebrated as a hero for saving Berthia's life. Both men are rightly celebrated as heroes for now working as suicide prevention advocates.

Their story raises important questions:

- Is it good that these men work in suicide prevention?
- Would it be equally as good if they worked in suicide assistance?
- Did Briggs do something right or something wrong by stopping Berthia's suicide?
- "Who gets suicide prevention and who gets suicide assistance?"[34]

That last question is one that authors Jonathon Van Maren and Blaise Alleyne have brought to the assisted suicide debate in the book *A Guide to Discussing Assisted Suicide*. Their point is that if someone supports assisted suicide because they believe in honoring the desire and choice of another, then the logical conclusion is that such an individual would have to support suicide assistance consistently for everyone who **wants** to die. But if we intervene in some cases, if we actively apply suicide prevention for some people—therefore overriding their desire, their choice to die—then we are showing the issue isn't really about choice; the issue is about judgment.

In other words, if we give suicide prevention to some, if we intervene and try to stop some suicides, then that is proof we are making a judgment that a particular individual's life is worth saving—that a particular individual's choice to die is worth overriding with our conviction to help them live. Correspondingly, then, when we assist with *some* suicides, we are making a judgment that those others are not lives worth saving.

Who are we to inconsistently make those judgments about others? Instead, wouldn't the most equitable approach, as Alleyne and Van Maren point out, be to either support suicide assistance for everyone or suicide prevention for everyone?

The idea that everyone should equally get suicide assistance generates an almost-universal visceral reaction of horror. And that's the point: It taps into peoples' intuition that if it would be wrong to give suicide assistance to everyone, then the most equitable alternative would ***not*** be suicide assistance to some, but rather would be suicide assistance to none.

Van Maren and Alleyne write the following:

> Most people who support assisted suicide also support suicide prevention. This is The Split Position... [which] considers suicide and assisted suicide as totally separate topics. People who hold to this position have often never tried to reconcile their conflicting beliefs. Our goal in responding to The Split Position in conversation is to attack this cognitive dissonance—to pit their own beliefs in preventing suicide and assisting suicide against each other, and show that The Split Position is a basic human rights violation because it splits people into protected and unprotected classes. Suicidal despair is always a symptom of some other unmet need. The desire to die is changeable, suicide prevention is a human right, suicide assistance is a human rights violation, and our moral duty to the suicidal is to prevent self-harm, never to facilitate it.[35]

When discussing this topic it is helpful to distinguish means from ends. The ***end*** of wanting someone to be pain-free is good. Whether or not the ***means*** to achieve that end is morally acceptable or not is entirely dependent on what the nature of the means is.

For example, wanting your child to attend university is a good end, but if the means to achieve that is the child lying about grades or you bribing the institution with money, that is not acceptable. Good end, yes, but not a good means. Analogously, then, it is possible to want someone's life to be free of suffering but it doesn't follow that all means to achieve that are ethical.

Consider for a moment what is at the heart of the belief system of civil societies: It is human equality.[36] When a society aims to be civil it develops human rights doctrines that acknowledge, for example, that people are equal because of their *nature* (human) rather than because of *some feature* they possess (e.g., age, ability, ethnicity, sex, or belief, to name a few).

Consider the United Nations' *Universal Declaration of Human Rights*, which was proclaimed by the UN General Assembly in 1948. It says the following:

> …recognition of the inherent dignity and of the equal and inalienable rights of all members of the human family is the foundation of freedom, justice and peace in the world...All human beings… are endowed with reason and conscience and should act towards one another in a spirit of brotherhood...Everyone has the right to life, liberty and security of person.[37]

What is a "spirit of brotherhood"? What is it about familial relationships that make them something worth modelling? It is the notion that humans are to be treated with kindness, respect, and charity; in other words, family members don't kill each other.

Consider, for a moment, what element of the 1994 Rwandan genocide was more horrifying than other human rights violations?[38] It was that colleagues, neighbors, friends—and even family—were turning over and killing people *that they knew*. It was not just a matter of strangers killing strangers (as horrific as that is). Consider the story of Rwandan genocide survivor Monica.[39] Her Tutsi husband and six children were brutally executed by her Hutu father and brothers. They did more than attack Monica's spouse and offspring. They attacked their bond with her. They attacked their relationship. They attacked the "spirit of brotherhood" that should exist in families, let alone all of humanity.

Or consider the story of Penny Boudreau, a woman from Nova Scotia, Canada, who strangled to death her 12-year-old daughter Carissa in 2008. The young victim's last words to the woman who birthed her were these: "Mommy, don't!"[40]

There is something horrifying about her second-last word in the context it was said: "Mommy." That little girl's word choice was making a profound appeal; her use of the term "Mommy" was a call to the nature of who Penny was—a mom. "Mommy, don't!" was a cry that is more about the first word than the second. It's more than ***Don't*** *kill me*. It was a shriek from the very depths of her being: ***Mommy!*** *Do what mommies do!* It was a cry for the spirit of brotherhood.
To maintain a "spirit of brotherhood" is to ensure we do not kill people. Whether it is mothers, fathers, sisters, brothers, or even strangers, the idea is that we should treat each other with a familial spirit; in other words, we should care and not kill.

Someone, however, might object. They might point out that if a family member wants to die due to unsolved suffering, then a spirit of brotherhood might involve killing *if* killing would give comfort to a loved one, if it would take away pain.

Whereas Mary from Rwanda or Carissa from Canada experienced betrayal from loved ones, is it possible that some familial killing would not be a betrayal but instead an act of mercy? After all, consider a family dog: if a beloved pet is sick and in pain and we can no longer help via veterinary means, then we do kill it to put it out of its misery. In that case, killing the dog is considered the most loving thing to do.

Likewise, someone might argue, we should generally not kill our relatives; however, if their suffering cannot be eliminated, shouldn't we "put them down" as we do beloved pets?

The short answer is that we don't treat Grandma like Buddy the dog because Grandma isn't a dog. After all, would we put grandma's food in a bowl on the floor and tell her to crawl on her hands and knees in order to eat it? Of course not—even though we do that for Buddy. Why? Because, simply put, they are ***different***.

While a pet can be nice companion, a being to sit close to, or a creature to aid someone living with a disability, pets are not humans. Pets are not our spouses. They are not our parents or our offspring. They are not business partners. They do not govern society with us. While pets should be treated with kindness, they are not our equals. Animals are subordinate to us rather than the other way around. That is not license to be cruel to them, but it is license to treat humans differently from how we treat animals. After all, when a cat kills a mouse we do not consider it a homicide worthy of investigation, but when a human kills a human, we do.

As it says in Genesis 1:26,

> Then God said: 'Let us make man in our image, after our likeness. Let them have ***dominion*** [emphasis added] over the fish of the sea, the birds of the air, and the cattle, and over all the wild animals and all the creatures that crawl on the ground.'

We are to be ***stewards*** of the earth, yes, but we are to ***love*** our neighbors (Matthew 22:39). It is our fellow humans who image God and it is therefore not the prerogative for the creature to end the life of someone who bears the image of the Creator ("You shall not kill" –Exodus 20:13).

Moreover, when we put a pet down, we do so because their usefulness in our lives is outweighed by harms (such as poor health that cannot be corrected at all or without great expense, or because there isn't a home for them and they will be a nuisance to society, etc.). Humans, however, should not be valued from the perspective of usefulness.

Consider, for example, why slavery is wrong. Slavery treats humans as objects; it values another based on performance, on what the other can do and provide and then uses and abuses the "product." To be against slavery is to be against treating humans as objects. To be against slavery is to be against valuing humans based on performance. To be against slavery is to see humans as subjects. To be against slavery is to value humans for who they are rather than what they do. To be against slavery is to see humans from the perspective of their ***being*** rather than their ***doing***; it is to see them as being image-bearers, to see them as beings to love and be loved by. When family pets are alive they do not always maintain their usefulness, but as long as family ***members*** are alive they always maintain their being.

Moreover, if we say that love of a relative would compel us to commit a "mercy killing" because the relative wants her suffering to end, then we are left with the great challenge mentioned earlier: Who decides which suffering gets suicide assistance versus other suffering which gets suicide prevention? ***All*** of our loved ones will suffer, so how do we decide which suffering should lead to killing and which should lead to searching for meaning? If the criteria for suicide assistance is merely that the person desires death, then relatives who may wish to die are not limited to kin who are elders. In fact, as I write this, a 27-year-old woman in Ontario, Canada, has spoken publicly about her desire for assisted suicide because she is suffering from Fibromyalgia, a non-fatal condition which has symptoms including widespread pain, fatigue, and cognitive difficulties.[41]

Where do we draw the line?

One might respond that the difference is that elders are closer to death. First, notice how quickly one criterion for suicide assistance ("The person wants it") expands to two criteria ("Okay, it's not just that the person wants it; they also have to be suffering") and then expands to three criteria ("Hmmm, okay they have to want it and be suffering, but they also have to be near death"). At the end of the day, the growing list of criteria reinforces that not everyone should be considered a candidate for suicide assistance—but some should. Continually adding to the requirements shows that judgments are being made as to what justifies acting in that manner, thus emphasizing that some lives are worth saving while others are not.

Second, another dilemma arises: How does one decide how close to death a person must be? Six months? Six weeks? Six days? Such criteria are always arbitrary and subjective.[42]

Third, what if the estimate is actually wrong? The father of one of my friends was told he had days left to live but three years later was living back home.

Fourth, even if one's death could be accurately estimated, why would closeness to death be license for killing? In fact, if someone is so miserable they want to die, wouldn't closeness to death be a consolation whereas distance from death be a further suffering? By that logic, one could reasonably deny the "almost dead" assisted suicide because their wish is about to unfold naturally, whereas those furthest from death would be more suitable candidates for assisted suicide because, without it, their unmet desire for death would be too long a road. Of course, I am not actually suggesting this should be our philosophy, but instead am exposing the flawed mindset for what it is—the use of killing to solve problems that can, and should, be addressed another way.

Fifth, when we create laws that allow for some suicide assistance, such as for those "closer" to death (whatever that means), there could be people who ask for assistance with suicide out of guilt. Elders, who are less able to do all the things they once did, may feel like a burden on those around them; instead of having their worth affirmed, a society that allows for assisted suicide could be just the climate that "guilts" such vulnerable individuals into asking for it. Sure, those individuals may claim to want assisted suicide, but deep down they are asking for it out of duty, thinking they *ought to* because others have done so already. Since death is permanent, shouldn't we err on the side of caution? In other words, if we had to choose between a society that either a) deprives someone of death precisely when he wants it, or b) gives someone death before he truly wants it, which should we pick? The person being "deprived" of assisted suicide will still get death—just not at his own, personally-calculated time. But the person being deprived of life will never get that living time back.[43]

Sixth, it is worth pointing out that where assisted suicide is legal, people in the medical community are the ones enlisted to execute it. Do we really believe that health care professionals, who have chosen a career aimed at curing or caring, should expand their "services" to killing? Consider the following: In 2016, *The New York Times* reported that the pharmaceutical company Pfizer "had imposed sweeping controls on the distribution of its products to ensure that none are used in lethal injections."[44] More than twenty other drug companies had done the same. And the American Medical Association also raised concerns, stating that "…requiring physicians to participate in executions violates their oath to protect lives and erodes public confidence in the medical profession."[45] Couldn't the same be said about health care workers' involvement in assisted suicide?[46] In other words, if the medical community should not be involved in ending guilty prisoners' lives, how much more should it not be involved in ending innocent patients' lives?

At this point, it would perhaps be good here to reflect on the question, "Why is suicide—assisted or solo—wrong?"

Suicide is wrong because it is a destructive solution to the universal human experience of suffering. It is wrong because it doesn't address the underlying problems that people feel are driving them to despair. It is wrong because it rejects the great good of life itself. It is wrong because it leaves a wake of brokenness for those left behind. As Sergeant Briggs wrote in his book, *Guardian of the Golden Gate: Protecting the Line Between Hope and Despair*, "Suicide ends one life, and it affects so many others. Jason [a young man who jumped from the bridge] ended his pain on July 22, 2013. He didn't intend it this way, but the pain for his parents was just beginning."[47] Suicide is wrong because it denies hope. As Briggs also wrote, "Hope is the single most important tool for anyone struggling with depression or mental illness—it can save lives. I've seen it happen over and over again, not just on the Bridge but in my experiences talking with people around the world."[48]

From a faith perspective, suicide is wrong because it is a rejection of the gift of life given by our good Heavenly Father. But what if someone responds this way: "If I no longer want a gift someone gave me for my birthday several years ago, it's okay for me to get rid of it, so isn't it okay for me to choose assisted suicide and get rid of my gift of life I no longer want?"[49]

To answer that, we need to realize the following: The gift of life we've been given is so valuable it's priceless. We're not talking about getting an article of clothing that will go out of style. Instead, imagine being given a billion dollars. It wouldn't make sense to use only a portion of it and say, "I don't want it anymore," and then proceed to burn the rest. So too would it be wrong to live a portion of our lives and then prematurely destroy them. So if we don't understand how valuable our lives are, then our job is to eliminate our incorrect understanding as to our worth, rather than eliminate our lives.

Moreover, think for a moment about the giver of the gift of life: The giver loves unconditionally and is perfect; He only wants our good. Therefore, His judgment is better than ours. He takes great joy in giving us the gift of life, knowing that it is life that is necessary to enter into a relationship of love—with Him and with others. Can you imagine throwing a present in the face of a parent who lovingly gives his child a toy that will bring happiness? How, then, could we throw back in the face of an all-good God the gift of life He gave us?

To be sure, life on this earth has a natural expiry date built into it due to sin introducing death into the world. To address that briefly, let's look at Genesis: 2:16-17: "The Lord God gave man this order: 'You are free to eat from any of the trees of the garden except the tree of knowledge of good and bad. From that tree you shall not eat; the moment you eat from it you are surely doomed to die.'" Sadly, Adam and Eve chose to not trust their loving Father's rule; they chose to disobey Him; they chose to sin. And yet, even in God's disappointment with his beloved creation's betrayal, there lies within God's response an act of mercy:

> Then the Lord God said, 'See! The man has become like one of us, knowing what is good and what is bad! Therefore, he must not be allowed to put out his hand to take fruit from the tree of life also, and thus eat of it and live forever.' The Lord God therefore banished him from the garden of Eden, to till the ground from which he had been taken. When he expelled the man, he settled him east of the garden of Eden; and he stationed the cherubim and the fiery revolving sword, to guard the way to the tree of life (Genesis 3:22-24).

In what way was God's prevention of Adam and Eve eating from the tree of life an act of mercy after the fall? Since man was separated from God by his sin, if Adam and Eve ate from the tree of life and lived forever, they would have lived eternally separated from their Creator. By protecting them from living forever at that moment, God was giving them a second chance, a chance for their broken relationship to be repaired first. But how could it be repaired? God who is ever-creative, took the terrible thing Adam and Eve did and redeemed it: Since the punishment for sin was death, God made man's redemption come through death too—Jesus' death. Jesus would take on the punishment that should be man's.

The "tree of life" in which they would live forever would come through God himself, becoming man in the form of Jesus, who would be nailed upon a tree, rise from the dead, and open the gates to Eternal Life.

So man would now be pilgrims on a journey, living a finite existence in which God, like a lover, would pursue His beloved and try to win them back. As we are told in Revelation 21:1-4,

> Then I saw a new heaven and a new earth. The former heaven and the former earth had passed away, and the sea was no more. I also saw the holy city, a new Jerusalem, coming down out of the heaven from God, prepared as a bride adorned for her husband. I heard a loud voice from the throne saying, 'Behold, God's dwelling is with the human race. He will dwell with them and they will be his people and God himself will always be with them [as their God]. He will wipe every tear from their eyes, and there shall be no more death or mourning, wailing or pain, [for] the old order has passed away.

So a new, suffering-free, life awaits us. But until that next chapter comes, we should carefully reverence the gift of life God has given us until it comes to its end. Having said that, some might interject that if someone is suffering they cannot "do" much with their gift, nor are they enjoying it, so what is the point?

When Viktor Frankl was imprisoned in concentration camps he saw some suffering people with this type of attitude who rejected the gift of their lives by committing suicide. He wrote about how he decided he would not follow in their footsteps and that he would try to dissuade others from giving up on life.

One of his insights was this: "…love is the ultimate and the highest goal to which man can aspire…*The salvation of man is through love and in love* …a man who has nothing left in this world still may know bliss, be it only for a brief moment, in the contemplation of his beloved."[50]

If there is no life, there can be no love. By respecting the gift of life, of an unknown duration, that each of us has been given, then we can love. Yes, we will love even better in eternity with God. If our Creator, however, in His wisdom has chosen for our lives to carry on for a little while longer on earth, we best steward that life by loving rather than taking control and doing things our own way like Adam and Eve did.

That reminds me of an exchange Sergeant Briggs had with a man wanting to jump off the Bridge. The individual was a wealthy businessman. His children went to private schools and he had both a home and a fancy car. But hard times fell upon him and he wasn't able to maintain that lifestyle. In despair, he went to the bridge to end his life. Sergeant Briggs asked him what his marriage was built on—material objects or love? The man responded that it was the latter. So Briggs followed it up with another question that became a game-changer: "If your wife lost her job or your child failed a class and was up here as you are, contemplating suicide, what would you say to them?"[51]

The man's response? "I don't have to think about it. I would tell them how much I love them, how important they are in my life, and how much I would miss them."[52]

When we embrace suicide, we remove the vehicle of our lives which is the necessary instrument through which we give and receive love.

In Matthew 25, Jesus speaks of His return and how He will reward those who loved Him through loving others. Jesus lists various examples of suffering souls and not once does he propose killing as the solution to their suffering. On the contrary, what elicits God's acclaim is the ***working against*** an individual's death, the fixing of a problem at its root, the manifestation of love:

> Then the king will say to those on his right, 'Come, you who are blessed by my Father. Inherit the kingdom prepared for you from the foundation of the world. For I was hungry and you gave me food, I was thirsty and you gave me drink, a stranger and you welcomed me, naked and you clothed me, ill and you

cared for me, in prison and you visited me….whatever you did for one of these least brothers of mine, you did for me' (Matthew 25: 34-36, 40).

3

Suffering Unleashes Love

In the summer of 2019, I sat down with the Grants[53], a family I have long admired. Their daughter Elizabeth[54] is a couple years younger than me and has endured many crosses from a declining health condition. I never got to know the Grants well, but when I think of each person in their family who I have had brief interactions with, I have the same impression of them all: Peaceful. Calm. Quiet. Kind.

And so, it was they who came to my mind when I sat down to write this book. I did an inventory of people I know who have endured great trials, and although I didn't know much, I knew enough to ask if theirs was a story they were willing to share.

When Mrs. Grant was six months pregnant with Elizabeth, she had a frightening premonition: As she hung the laundry one day, she was seized with a sense that the child she was carrying would have a disability. When Elizabeth was born, it did not appear the fear would become reality. Elizabeth was developing as expected; that is, until around 13 months. She started to walk just after turning a year old but would fall down in a way her mom felt was abnormal. She stopped speaking at the age of six. Her physical condition declined so that she needed a walker, and then a wheelchair. Soon she no longer had the muscle-tone to drive her own wheelchair. Today, at 37, Elizabeth is entirely dependent on others for her survival.

She is tube fed because she chokes. She cannot speak or write. She has no strength to even turn herself over in bed. And so, every night, her 69 and 77-year-old parents will take turns, waking up, going to her room, and turning over her 120-pound body so she does not experience discomfort and bed sores. If Elizabeth is itchy, she cannot tell anyone. If a strand of hair is stuck in her mouth to great annoyance, she cannot move it nor ask for someone to do so. She can and will cry out. Then, her parents must guess—and wait—to figure out what the problem is and try to solve it.

I asked Mr. Grant how they handle the 24-hour care with limited respite. I appreciated his honesty. Their family has long been admired by many in their church as a beautiful witness of patience, endurance, and love. But that doesn't mean it has come easily. It doesn't mean they have some supernatural capacity to live their story void of the human experiences of grief, pain, and confusion at times.

"We're tired," he said wearily.

One of the hardest things, he candidly admitted, is being at church, and hearing a Scripture reference about people being healed. It pierces his heart. "Why not us?" he wonders. "Why isn't Elizabeth healed? Why isn't our prayer answered?"

I asked how he responds to his own questions. He quoted for me from John 6:68: "to whom shall we go?"

In the Gospel of John, Jesus gives a hard teaching to His followers. He declares, "I am the living bread that came down from heaven; whoever eats this bread will live forever; and the bread that I will give is my flesh for the life of the world" (John 6:51). The crowd does not take too kindly to this seemingly bizarre proclamation. The Scriptures say, "The Jews quarreled among themselves, saying, 'How can this man give us [his] flesh to eat?'" (John 6:52). Jesus reiterates His claim and two things happen:

1) Some disciples declare, "This saying is hard" (John 6:60).
2) Some take action: "As a result of this, many [of] his disciples returned to their former way of life and no longer accompanied

him" (John 6:66).

This became a defining moment. Jesus looked at his closest companions, the 12 apostles, and asked a question (John 6:67):

"Do you also want to leave?"

Suffering can become a similar defining moment. Do we want to leave and will we indeed do so?

Mr. Grant knew his family's suffering, and the lack of healing, was their defining moment: Would they leave?

And Mr. Grant responded as Simon Peter did: "Master, to whom shall we go? You have the words of eternal life. We have come to believe and are convinced that you are the Holy One of God" (John 6:68-69).

When humans experience suffering, it can be tempting to question the greatness of God. It can be tempting to leave. But if we do, where else shall we go?

If someone were to reject God, what is the alternative? Certainly running to Satan would be of no help. Satan made no personal sacrifices for humanity. Satan did not compose the Bible to proclaim a message of Good News. Satan has no interest in helping people. Whereas God delights in the creation and flourishing of humans, Satan revels in the attack and destruction of humans.

One might suggest we disregard Satan—and God—entirely, and say there is no higher power at all. But how does that position explain the complexities of creation? Consider a priceless painting—it doesn't just fall from the sky. As a painting requires a painter, design requires a designer. The intelligent design of nature, let alone creatures themselves, points to an intelligent designer—in other words, God. Sure, it takes faith to believe in God, but it also takes faith to believe the complexities of our world came from nothing. Since both options require faith, it makes more sense to conclude design comes from a designer rather than randomness. Of course, much more could be, and has been, said about proving the existence of God, and of Jesus as God in particular, but since that is not the purpose of this book, I leave the point there.[55]

If the idea of "no God" is an option that is not logical, if the idea of leaving God for Satan is an option rooted in misery, wouldn't the wisest choice be to side with the idea that there is a good and loving God who is all-knowing in a way we are not and that there is nowhere else for us to go? It is to trust that God sees what we do not.

As we are told in Isaiah 55:8-9, "'For my thoughts are not your thoughts, nor are your ways my ways,' says the Lord. 'As high as the heavens are above the earth, so high are my ways above your ways and my thoughts above your thoughts.'"

Therefore, when suffering occurs and we cannot understand how a good God would not intervene in the way we would, we can remind ourselves of the following: 1) We don't see the full picture; 2) We are creature and not Creator; 3) Faith is trusting in the goodness of God even when our present circumstances leave our minds bewildered.

Consider a child demanding something delightful to the taste buds, like candy. If the parent says no to the sweet treat, the child may throw a tantrum and feel the parent isn't loving. But what if there are things the parent knows and sees that the child cannot comprehend?

What if the parent knows the child has a severe allergy and that a particular food choice would be harmful? What if the parent knows the child needs to grow in self-control and discipline and that denying the object of desire is good for her overall maturity? What if the parent is saving the candy for another person who was already promised it? What if the parent *is* going to give the child candy, but the "no" is a "no, not right now" because the parent wants the child to be ***extra delighted*** when she does finally receive what she asked for?

The point is, the young child simply does not comprehend all that the mature parent does. But if the parent is good, and loving, and kind, then we can at least trust that when the candy is withheld, there are good reasons. Not knowing the reasons should not cause us to conclude the parent is mean; rather, they should cause us to conclude that the child is not all-knowing.

So what can one do when overwhelmed by suffering and wanting to express deep sorrow while still trusting God? We can make God's Word our words. We can remember that even in the Scriptures there are prayers of lamentation which we can recite in order to find ways to verbalize the cry of our hearts. But let us also remember that effective communication is a two-way street, so when we cry out to God we ought to listen for His responses and allow these to settle into our souls and become our new "heartsong"[56]:

Our Lamentations	God's Answer
"My God, my God, why have you forsaken me?" –Matthew 27:46	"Can a mother forget her infant, be without tenderness for the child of her womb? Even should she forget, I will never forget you." –Isaiah 49:15
"Out of the depths I call to you, Lord; Lord, hear my cry!" –Psalm 130:1-2	"I will be with you as I was with Moses: I will not leave you nor forsake you." –Joshua 1:5
"Have pity on me, Lord, for I am weak; heal me, Lord, for my bones are trembling…I am wearied with sighing; all night long tears drench my bed; my couch is soaked with weeping." –Psalm 6:3,7	"The Lord is my shepherd; there is nothing I lack. In green pastures you let me graze; to safe waters you lead me; you restore my strength." –Psalm 23:1-3
"Lord, hear my prayer; listen to my cry for help. In this time of trouble I call." –Psalm 86:6-7	"O Lord, my God, I cried out to you and you healed me. Lord, you brought me up from Sheol; you kept me from going down to the pit." –Psalm 30:3-4
"For I know my offense; my sin is always before me. Against you alone have I sinned; I have done such evil in your sight." –Psalm 51:5-6	"I will sprinkle clean water upon you to cleanse you from all your impurities… I will give you a new heart and place a new spirit within you, taking from your bodies your stony hearts and giving you natural hearts." –Ezekiel 36:25-26

"In her bitterness she prayed to the Lord, weeping copiously…I am an unhappy woman…" –1 Samuel 1:10, 15	"Go in peace, and may the God of Israel grant you what you have asked of him." –1 Samuel 1:17
"Will the Lord reject us forever, never again show favor? Has God's love ceased forever? Has the promise failed for all ages? Has God forgotten mercy, in anger withheld compassion? –Psalm 77:8-10	"When you call me, when you go to pray to me, I will listen to you. When you look for me, you will find me. Yes, when you seek me with all your heart, you will find me with you, says the Lord, and I will change your lot." –Jeremiah 29:12-14

Sometimes terrible things have a mysterious way of being blessings in disguise. Several years ago, my friend Magda was excitedly preparing to go on a trip to France. About five or six days before her flight, she threw one of her vests in the laundry and forgot her passport was in the pocket. She was devastated! More than that, she was hugely upset *at God* for permitting it. Magda rushed out to a Service Canada office to see if she could get an expedited passport (she could). Once there, she found out that France requires at least six months passport validity for entry to their country, and that her passport had had only two months left. In other words, had her passport *not* been destroyed, its impending expiry would have been discovered at the airport instead, and her long anticipated France vacation is what would have been destroyed.

Or, to use another example, on one of my many trips, I heard a story from a woman who gave a testimony at a church I was visiting. She spoke about how, when she was pregnant, she developed complications that required she be hospitalized. During her stay, a more serious problem was discovered—one that would have left her dead had she not been in the right environment where medical personnel could immediately respond. In other words, the suffering of her pregnancy complication led her to the hospital which is what ended up saving her from being killed by another problem. This experience brings to mind the insight of singer-songwriter Laura Story who composed, "…what if your blessings come through raindrops? What if your healing comes through tears? What if a thousand sleepless nights are what it takes to know you're near? What if trials of this life are your mercies in disguise?"[57]

Laura wrote that song, *Blessings*, in response to her husband developing a brain tumor and facing all kinds of health and life challenges as a result. Their world was turned upside down and their prayers for his healing were not answered as they wished.

In an interview she said, "Life is filled with things you don't expect, but the Bible tells us to respond by trusting God and continuing to worship him... God has proven to be faithful. We have been truly blessed out of a circumstance that at first didn't seem like much of a blessing at all."[58]

So if, in the face of suffering, we aren't going to go away from God, if we are to trust in His goodness even when suffering itself isn't good, how do we make any sense out of suffering?

I think one of the best answers to that can be found in a little booklet written by a Roman Catholic pope, John Paul II. In *Salvifici Doloris, on the Christian Meaning of Human Suffering*, he observed the following:

> We could say that suffering... [is] present in order *to unleash love in the human person*, that unselfish gift of one's 'I' on behalf of other people, especially those who suffer. The world of human suffering unceasingly calls for, so to speak, another world: the world of human love; and in a certain sense man owes to suffering that unselfish love that stirs in his heart and actions.[59]

Suffering unleashes love.

Elizabeth's suffering unleashed her family's love. Her parents, siblings, nieces, and nephews have learned to be more patient, more inclusive, and more tender.

In 2014, the suffering of my friend Jocelyn's dad unleashed her love. I met Jocelyn in 2005 when I moved to Calgary, Alberta; she was one of my first friends in the new city and has remained a faithful one, even as geography has spread us apart. Over the next 7 years of living there, Jocelyn was a true friend who shared in all kinds of adventures, highs, and lows. The year before I moved away, I started having sharp pains in my abdomen that led to two ultrasounds in one week to try to discover the problem (which, thankfully, amounted to nothing). I remember writhing in pain in bed one night while my roommate was away. Jocelyn came to the rescue and took care of me like she had a lifetime of nursing experience (except, instead, she had 18 years' experience as a videographer for a television station). I personally felt, on a small scale, Jocelyn's nurturing nature and charism to care for the sick; and it was that which, two years later, she would bestow on a large scale on one of the most important people in her life.

In 2014, Jocelyn's dad Normand was nearing the end of his battle with cancer. In late August of that year, Jocelyn got a call from one of her brothers:

"I think you should come home," he said.

"Are you telling me I need to come home?" she responded, acknowledging the code-language they were speaking—communicating that "Dad is near death" without actually saying it.

She got in her car, making the several-hour drive north. Her dad didn't leave the earth that weekend, so neither did Jocelyn leave her parents' farm. Instead, she would spend two months round-the-clock caring for her dad at the end of his life the way he once cared for her at the beginning of hers. Taking time off work in order to be the main caregiver for her father was not something she had to think about. It was a conviction in the depths of her being. She simply *knew* that's what she would do. And she did.

Normand couldn't be left alone because he would attempt to get himself up and, if no one was there, he would fall. So Jocelyn was the primary person at his bedside for the duration of the days while her mom was primary for nights (with other family and friends being a loving presence as well). Normand wanted to stay home, and Jocelyn's mom preferred that too, not only giving him his wishes but avoiding a 40-minute drive each way to the closest palliative care center. Because Jocelyn took time off work, her availability was an essential supplement to the care that her mom and siblings were already giving to her dad, and was *the* reason Normand could stay at home.

And what did that consist of? Holistically attending to him with the gift of presence and unconditional love and attention. Sitting beside her sleeping father. Being in the room with him when he was awake. Helping him walk from bed to chair. Adjusting him when he was uncomfortable. Holding his hand. Pushing him outside in his wheelchair. Putting a blanket on him. Telling him she loved him. Being silent with him. Crying. Laughing. Feeding him. Providing his pills. Celebrating another birthday with him. Buttoning his sweaters. It was a series of seemingly-little things that were actually huge for someone who could no longer do much for himself. Together, these made for a massive gesture of love. Jocelyn was entirely integrated into her father's days and fully attuned to his needs. Her gift of time made for a true "communion of persons."

Jocelyn said,

> I think I'm grateful that I was able to have that time with my dad, the intimacy of it, but also, I don't want to say share in the suffering but, to be present with him in that suffering, and learn from him until the end. He was still teaching me things, a lot of things, through that time....he was still very present. A lot of people thought he was out of it but he totally wasn't.

Because Jocelyn was providing such constant care, she had a keen sense of his needs and subtle communications. She could pick up on what he was trying to express in ways others couldn't, which was important for her dad. Being attuned to his life and his suffering is what made her respond with the gift of time and tender affection.

In 1962, Rick Hoyt's suffering unleashed his dad's (and mom's) love. It was that year when Rick was born. Due to being deprived of oxygen at birth, Rick was forever changed. He would live with spastic quadriplegia cerebral palsy.[60] His parents, Dick and Judy Hoyt, vowed to care for him, showering him in love and opportunity (which included Rick working hard and getting a university degree). They rejected the recommendation that they institutionalize him.

As the years went on, Dick and Rick have partnered up for marathons, triathlons, and even Ironmans. Son sits in a wheelchair (or dinghy), and dad pushes (or pulls). Even when Dick had a heart attack, not long after his recovery he was back running with his son.[61] Their story is all over the internet, having received millions of views, and is a constant source of inspiration for people world-wide.

In 2013, they received the Jimmy V Perseverance Award. In his acceptance speech, Dick declared,

> Rick is my inspiration. He has taught me great many things over the years. And every day I consider myself lucky to be his father and teammate...Next time you see someone in a wheelchair, or who can't talk or walk, or they may talk or walk a little bit different, they are people too, and deserve to be able to live, learn, work, and play.[62]

Rick's acceptance speech, spoken through a computer, was a powerful indication of the fruit of someone who received love in the face of suffering: "Yes you can," he told the audience, imparting Team Hoyt's motto. "Don't give up," he quoted from the award's namesake, "Don't ever give up."[63]

The concept of suffering unleashing love is also demonstrated in the friendship of Justin Skeesuck and Patrick Gray.[64] These two men have been lifelong friends, and their brotherhood only strengthened when tragedy struck—Justin developed a progressive neuromuscular disease and it deteriorated to the point that he now needs a wheelchair. Rather than wallowing in misery, Justin has demonstrated remarkable resilience and determination, which included fulfilling a desire to do The Camino de Santiago. In 2014, the men trekked "The Way of St. James" in a truly profound story of community, suffering, opportunity, and love. The Camino is a challenge at the best of times. Now imagine inserting a wheelchair into the picture.

I'll Push You: Embracing God's Promise of Provision is a 1-hour presentation on YouTube about their journey. In it, they reveal the ripple-effect of suffering unleashing love. Justin's suffering unleashed Patrick's love to even go on the journey. Then, while travelling, they faced backbreaking suffering in the form of having to navigate all kinds of mountainous, rough, muddy terrain, and it unleashed all sorts of love from fellow pilgrims who began as strangers but became like family as they helped them on their life-changing trek.

When talking about their experience, Justin and Patrick share a powerful story of a fellow traveler named Claudia who had helped them various times over a two-week period.

Claudia's story is a reminder that everyone on the Camino carries more than a backpack; they carry a personal story which is their reason for being there. Claudia's was particularly traumatic. Only half a year prior, on December 31, 2013, she had been home with family in South Africa. They were fulfilling their New Year's Eve tradition by setting up a camera for a family photo, doing the countdown, and capturing an image at midnight. "10, 9, 8…" they shouted. But when their countdown landed at 1, masked gunmen burst into their home and Claudia's dad was murdered in front of her eyes.[65]

Needless to say, she was walking the Camino filled with great anger and pain. In short, she was suffering. And yet, even in her hurt, she enjoyed helping Justin, Patrick, and their ever-growing team. One day they were working to get Justin in his wheelchair up a particularly steep cliff and in order to unite the team's effort, Justin began a countdown: "10, 9, 8…" You can only imagine the trigger that was for poor Claudia. The numbers brought her back to the trauma that countdowns had become for her. It was agony. She didn't want to hear those numbers. Not like that. Not again. She was suffering.

She nonetheless carried forward in helping the team push Justin. Later she journaled that upon summiting, where she and the others were joyfully celebrating their accomplishment, she was moved to tears because "I didn't believe that a countdown from 10 could ever be happy again."[66]

Claudia recalled an exchange she had with Justin that evening, when the team was spending time together as a brilliant sunset lit up the sky: "Justin looks at me and says, 'Thanks for getting me up that hill today.' I look back at him and say, 'No, Justin, it was *you* who got me up that hill'"[67]

Every person, in some way, is suffering, and with that reality comes all kinds of opportunities to unleash love. Proof of this isn't only in stories told on a grand scale to the world through presentations and popular online videos. Proof of it is also found on a small scale, in our everyday lives. When I went through my broken engagement, my suffering unleashed my cousin Belinda's love (amongst many others). Several weeks after my heartbreak, I left town for a 5-day business trip. When I returned I was surprised to learn that Belinda had spent that whole time completely transforming my basement suite. She knew my ex-fiancé had spent so much time visiting me that she wanted to give the place a brand new look. She turned it into an absolute oasis that definitely could have qualified for an *HGTV* home makeover success story. I was suffering, and it drew out of her great love. Not only did she sacrifice her time and her money that week, but she did it all while going through a flare up of her rheumatoid arthritis.

As I write this, I have a friend going through the worst post-partum depression I've ever witnessed, so severe that she had to be hospitalized a couple times in order to get the right help. And her suffering unleashed all kinds of love from visits to meals to money to support to counsel to babysitting to prayers, you name it, from friends, family, the medical community, and her husband who tirelessly rallied around her.

The idea that suffering unleashes love is a concept that is present in more than the stories above. It is a concept at the heart of the Gospel message. Consider the Scripture passage most commonly held up on poster board at sports games: John 3:16. What exactly does that passage say? "For God so loved the world that he gave his only Son, so that everyone who believes in him might not perish but might have eternal life."

When original sin entered the world through Adam and Eve's choice to disobey, humanity was separated from God. "For the wages of sin is death" (Romans 6:23). God, however, did not leave us in that suffering state. In His majesty and creativity He let our suffering unleash His love. He sent His only Son to enter into the human experience and, although Jesus was innocent, He would endure our punishment for sin. He would be tortured and killed. He would take the place for us. Then, He would rise from the dead and open the gates of Heaven so that we could have eternal life. Our suffering unleashed God's love. And that love restores us back to life: "…the gift of God is eternal life in Christ Jesus our Lord" (Romans 6:23).

Instead of someone's suffering unleashing assisted suicide, what if we focused on their suffering unleashing love? That love can take all kinds of forms. It may mean holding someone's hand while listening to beautiful music. It may mean reading to them because they can no longer see. It may mean playing a board game with them. It may mean transcribing their life lessons as their legacy to leave behind. It may mean acting as interpreter to their blinking eyes, which is their only way to communicate. It may mean changing their soiled diaper. It may mean gently wiping drool off their face. It may mean doing what my friend Josh did when his grandma was dying from cancer which had riddled her body and left her emaciated—he simply, yet powerfully, crawled into bed and curled up next to her in a gesture that spoke more than words ever could, an act of pure love that communicated, "You are not alone."

In 2019, two major media personalities appeared together. *CNN*'s Anderson Cooper interviewed comedian Stephen Colbert. Both men lost their fathers when they were just 10 years old. In Colbert's case, his dad died in a plane crash alongside two of Colbert's brothers. When speaking to Anderson about this he said,

> What do you get from loss? You get awareness of other peoples' loss. Which allows you to connect with that other person. Which allows you to love more deeply ... And so, at a young age I suffered something so that by the time I was in serious relationships in my life, with friends, or with my wife or with my children, is that I have some understanding that everybody is suffering. And, however imperfectly, acknowledge their suffering, and to connect with them and to love them in a deep way that not only accepts that all of us suffer, but also then makes you grateful for the fact that you have suffered—so that you can know that about other people…it's about the fullness of your humanity…[68]

Consider his words in light of the Gospel, and they become even more powerful than they already are! God did not create humans and remain far removed from them. No. Instead He fully entered into the human experience by becoming man. He experienced suffering and anguish like everyone else. Just as you or I can connect with others who suffer because of our own suffering, so too does God connect with us in a profoundly personal way—suffering to him is not just an idea, it was something He experienced through Jesus.

4

We Can Alleviate Suffering without Eliminating Sufferers

It was an encounter science predicted would never happen. As I sat sipping coffee, my interviewee, a 30-year-old teaching assistant, enjoyed a Root Beer, masking the reality that he normally received nutrition by a feeding tube. But I guess Root Beer isn't really nutritious. I suppose if you're going to ingest it, you may as well let it serve its only purpose—to treat the taste buds.[69]

Moe Tapp[70] was "supposed" to be dead 28 years ago. But sometimes people defy the odds. I learned about his condition two years before learning about him. Epidermolysis Bullosa (EB) is something I tell my audiences about when I speak on assisted suicide and suffering. I often tell the story of Jonathan Pitre[71], a teenager who lived for 18 years with the excruciatingly painful condition, and I talk about how killing people ought **not** be the solution when we need to kill pain.

And then, one day, a person with EB showed up in my audience: Moe was grateful someone was telling others about *"**the worst disease you've never heard of**,"*[72] as an EB organization describes it.

When we subsequently met at an A&W in downtown Vancouver for him to tell me his story, I reacted the way most do when they encounter someone whose skin is as fragile as a butterfly's wings, whose painful blisters cover a majority of his bandaged body: "Is it okay to hug you?" I cautiously asked, not wanting the pressure of a hug to inflict pain.

"Yes," he said. "Don't worry. If it would hurt me, trust me, I wouldn't let you." He does, though, have a fear of falling and typically needs assistance walking down stairs to ensure he doesn't fall—because he has, and there aren't words to describe the searing pain of blistered skin slamming against hard floor.

It has been said that "Two people can look at the exact same thing and see something totally different," which demonstrates that "Perspective is everything." That is certainly true when considering Moe's story.

One could focus on Moe's bedtime routine: How he connects his feeding tube so liquid nutrients can be slowly dripped into him while he sleeps.

But better would be to focus on what Moe wakes up for: his employment at a high school where he works with students from grades 8-12 who have learning issues of all kinds, whether ADHD, dyslexia, autism, etc. His own experience of suffering, and rising above it, gives him profound compassion. He is fulfilled in being needed by his students, who are fulfilled by him connecting with them, by his belief in them and their ability to achieve.

Moe could be frustrated by the stares and questions he gets about why he looks different, and whether or not he was burned in a fire or car crash.

But instead he seizes the inquiries as opportunities to raise awareness about EB. As Moe said, *"We won't find a cure if people don't care, and people won't care if people don't know."* Moe confidently initiates discussion of his condition every year with a new crop of students. He encourages their inquisitiveness. In doing so, he not only teaches them about his condition, he teaches them how to be accepting of one's differences.

One could focus on the brief period of anger Moe went through in his mid-twenties. Blisters in his throat caused such severe pain he couldn't eat at all by mouth. He realized then that he would never be able to be spontaneous and just go travelling without doing weeks of research to make sure all he needed could be addressed in a new environment.

But better would be to focus on the camp he went to in Minnesota where anyone in the world who has a skin disease is invited to gather. He first went as an attendee and then returned as a volunteer. Knowing he was part of a broader community of people whose shared experience enabled them to readily empathize with each other gave him encouragement. Attendees cheered each other on with this philosophy: ***"If you can do this, if you can overcome, so can I."***

One could spend time dwelling on the burden and pain of baths and dressing changes every 2-3 days that cost $1,000/month—and the infections and exhaustion that come along with living with EB.

But better would be to reflect on how his Catholic Christian faith has sustained him (and become more personal and real for him in adulthood), and how his family and friends have rallied around him and stood by his side. Moe is a gamer. He also loves watching wrestling (and dreams of being a commentator for pro-wrestling). Old school Rock and Roll is his music genre of choice and reading is also on his list of enjoyable activities.

Moe has never thought of suicide. But on that topic, and its close relative euthanasia, he said he does understand why people would consider them due to pain—not that he supports them; in fact, he views both as wrong and would instead focus on pain relief and comfort. He noted that he became convinced euthanasia was wrong when he heard a compelling pro-life presentation; he realized that to say someone like him should be allowed assisted suicide, but others should not, is to make the judgment that his life is somehow less valuable than someone who is nondisabled. He said if someone wanted to end their life he would ask why, then see what their life was like at home, at school, etc., and then work to make that person's life better.

"There's hope, always hope," he declared. "I know it sounds corny, but it's true. People will always be around you that care."

Of course, if such people are lacking, it would be better to ***introduce supportive people*** rather than ***eliminate a suffering person***. Moe himself has reached out to families whose babies are diagnosed with EB. They first connect over the condition, but remain friends because of a familial bond that forms.

At the beginning of the interview I asked Moe how he would describe himself. "Good natured," he said. "[A] good dude, pretty chill." That definitely captures my observation of him; and when I think of that, plus the full and satisfying life he leads, even with—and perhaps because of—such a debilitating condition, I think about how, in a paradoxical way, Moe Tapp is comfortable in his skin.

What's notable about Moe's story is that his pain and suffering have not been entirely eliminated; however, his joy and fulfillment in life are proof that even when we cannot eliminate suffering we can alleviate it.

If, on the contrary, we eliminate people whose suffering we do not yet know how to fix, what motivation would we have to come up with better pain management, and so forth? My friend Dr. Will Johnston, a family physician, once wisely remarked, "When you see only death as a solution you throw creativity out of the window. Medical diligence goes out the window. The need to actually solve the problem, the need to actually examine the patient, and find a solution, goes out the window."[73]

Consider how different our world would be if, one hundred or more years ago, when diabetics were dying for lack of insulin, society euthanized them? There is a big difference between killing as the solution, and death as the problem. With the former, we are less motivated to come up with other solutions because we have found one. But with the latter, it's the lack of solution that becomes motivation for getting creative. Indeed, people dying from diabetes became a motivating factor to develop insulin, which is a game-changer for people suffering from that condition.

Other ways of getting creative and being solution-oriented is to focus on disability supports, like home care/personal support staff, accessible housing, mobility devices, accessible transit, accommodations for sensory disabilities (audiobooks, hearing aids) and peer support.

Having said that, as much as we should work to alleviate suffering without eliminating sufferers, we cannot stave off death forever. Proponents of assisted suicide may characterize opponents of it as people who want to keep others alive on this earth forever. That is simply not true. Opponents of assisted suicide recognize death is inevitable. It is just that we don't believe in inflicting suicide or homicide as a means to bring about that death; instead, we believe in letting nature take its course while offering comfort that addresses the whole person.[74]

This is what palliative care does, which is a great alternative to assisted suicide. Consider this definition by the World Health Organization:

> Palliative care is an approach that improves the quality of life of patients and their families facing the problem associated with life-threatening illness, through the prevention and relief of suffering by means of early identification and impeccable assessment and treatment of pain and other problems, physical, psychosocial and spiritual.[75]

The point is that even when cures don't exist, comfort and quality care are possible. When we handle peoples' suffering properly, they are unlikely to request assisted suicide. Consider the words of Jean Echlin, RN, MScN,

> With 26 years[']experience as a palliative care nurse specialist and consultant[,] I have been at the bedside of more than one thousand dying individuals. Thus, I can assure you that persons who receive timely, appropriate and expert pain and symptom management, including attention to significant socio-spiritual, psychological and emotional issues, do not ask for assisted suicide or euthanasia. With the inclusion of family members as the 'unit of care,' people want to live as long as possible! In fact, good hospice/palliative care can actually extend the life span. As well, it gives patients an improved quality of life at the end of life.[76]

An audience member taught me the truth of that statement with her lived experience: She told me about a colleague she had befriended while working at Walmart. The colleague developed spinal cancer, was in the end stages, and facing excruciating pain. So overwhelmed by her condition, she filled out paperwork for assisted suicide. She needed a witness to sign the document, and asked her friend to sign. The woman told me she looked compassionately at her suffering friend and gently said, "I can't do that." She then sat down on her friend's bed and tenderly asked, "What are you most afraid of?" The woman said, "The pain!" She was already enduring great suffering and feared it only getting worse.

Her friend asked about them consulting palliative care pain specialists to see what options were available to her as it worsened, and discovered helpful interventions existed that didn't have to include suicide assistance. The friend promised to continue visiting the woman, and when she did, would wrap her arms around her and give the gift of presence and touch. She knew the dying woman loved butterflies and she would say to her, "Imagine yourself soaring with the butterflies." The woman said that even though she was suffering "there are still moments of joy." Because she decided to reject suicide assistance, she experienced those moments of joy; she was helped by the medical advances of pain relief; she knew the comfort of a colleague who demonstrated true compassion—"to suffer together." The woman passed away naturally within a week, knowing the loving presence of her sons and that colleague who cared enough to say no to suicide assistance and to help create an alternative solution.

Some might object, however, and say, "But was that worth it? Shouldn't she still be allowed the choice? What if her suffering went on longer? What if she didn't change her mind?" Chapter 2 provided answers to that response.

Instead of using the unethical means of killing to achieve the end result of ending someone's suffering, the key is to surround people with consolation until death comes for them, and good palliative care makes that possible. One of my childhood best friends, Julia, became a family physician and also does some work in hospice. In a presentation to teenagers on the topic of assisted suicide she shared,

> I think it is possible for people to have a 'good' death. I think of my patients who come to the hospice when it is clear that their

cancer is not going to be cured. They may choose not to have further treatment, based on the side effects. [This is an important point. Patients can still refuse interventions that are disproportionate, even if they don't believe in assisted suicide.] Once at the hospice, they have their own room. They are surrounded by their families until the end. They can accept what is happening and face it with peace, even though it is always sad to say goodbye. Nurses are present to try to ease their pain and take care of their needs. I think of the time they have talking to their loved ones. When you know that your time is limited, each conversation is more meaningful. Each moment together matters. Families will not forget those moments.

Palliative care is not easy—it requires people to be creative, like helping people redefine their goals. Sometimes if a parent has a terminal illness, this means helping them write letters to their children to be opened at specific times—like high school graduation. Even though the parent longs to be there in person, they can still be present through a meaningful letter.[77]

Julia's remarks about patients using whatever time they have left to leave an intentional legacy for their loved ones remind me of my friend Alex who I write about in the epilogue. Alex was a young father who died of cancer; rather than shortening his life with assisted suicide, he maximized his time by preparing until illness finally stopped the clock. His wife Elaine wrote,

> One of the kindest things Alex did as we started to prepare intentionally for his absence was that he gathered a group of men from family, school and church and shared with them the burdens of his heart and some of the practical needs he felt they could meet once he was gone. He gave them very concrete ways in which he wanted them to help, from assisting me with some household tasks to encouraging the children as they grew older. I can only imagine how difficult this must have been as he contemplated all the moments when he would not be there, and I was so proud of the courage and grace he showed in that moment.[78]

Or take the insights of Dr. BJ Miller, a hospice and palliative care physician who gave a *TED Talk* in 2015. He remarked,

> Since dying is a necessary part of life, what might we create with this fact? ...I am asking we make space, physical, psychic room to allow life to play itself all the way out, so that rather than getting out of the way, aging and dying can become a process of crescendo through to the end.[79]

Crescendo! As a musician, I love this illustration. When playing music, anything marked with crescendo means you are to gradually increase the volume. Too often we view death and dying as fizzling out rather than as an epic orchestral ending. Understandably, the reality of disease and dying doesn't mean people will necessarily be *showing* a crescendo externally. Death can be very hard—in fact, even brutal at times. The question is, how can we make a crescendo happen internally? How can we be intentional about the environment a dying person is in (make it beautiful), the people they are surrounded by (have them be tender), and the conversations and reflections that occur (make them healing) so that one's ending can be a crescendo from that perspective?

Dr. Miller also said, "Let death be what takes us, not lack of imagination."[80] With assisted suicide, death doesn't take us—we take death, and when we do that, people die for lack of imagination; they die for lack of a creative response to the suffering they are facing. In contrast, palliative care is about using our imagination and getting creative. Julia addressed this when she spoke to those teenagers:

> I would like to challenge each of you today to think about how you can be defenders of life. One of the most important things that sick people need is companionship. People fear abandonment even more than pain. So if you know someone who is unwell or in a hospital or nursing home—visit them. Get to know them. If you feel awkward or don't know what to say, just be present. Think about when you were a kid and your mom or dad sat by when you were sick—something about them being there was comforting. Pray for the people you visit. Read to them or listen to music with them. I think of the character in the book *Still Alice* who loves ice cream. Even as her memory fails

because of dementia, she continues to enjoy the experience of eating an ice cream cone. Find out what people enjoy and make it possible.

When you're thinking about your future career, consider how you can help improve the lives of sick, disabled, or vulnerable people. This could mean working directly in health care, but the possibilities are broader than that—think of interior designers who make nursing homes more beautiful, or chefs who prepare meals for patients in a hospice, or engineers who design new equipment to keep people mobile, or administrators who organize volunteers to visit the elderly.[81]

So, we should get creative; we should replace assisted suicide with more and better palliative care. But what about some specifics? Since death is a part of life, when illness arises, how does one make ethical decisions that neither hasten nor prolong death? There are various resources that go into great depth about the nitty gritty of ethical decision making at end-of-life, and the purpose of this book is not that. However, I will propose a few questions to ask that highlight general principles we should keep in mind:

A. Is my behavior reflective of respecting the dignity of the person and their life?

When deciding what treatments to begin, continue, or cease, it is important that our underlying disposition be one of seeing the patient's life as valuable, independent of their abilities or productivity. Referring to an individual as a "vegetable" or a "drain on resources" would be dehumanizing language that ought to be rejected. Our attitude should be one of seeing them as image-bearers, individuals to love and be loved by. If this is the universal starting place, then it's easier to have discussions about what interventions should or should not be done because you know all parties are working from this life-affirming foundation. But if some people come from the perspective that humans may be killed, it is impossible to trust their judgment on the ethics of intervening because their worldview is fundamentally flawed.

B. Is the person's desire ordered or disordered?

It does not follow, by the mere existence of a wish, that we should fulfill it. After all, what if the wish is disordered? Consider the condition Body Integrity Identity Disorder (BIID), where people with healthy body parts are convinced, in their minds, that they should be disabled in some way (some with BIID desire to become amputees even though there is no presence of a pathology that would warrant amputation). By this example we can see that we humans have all sorts of desires; some of our desires are ordered (such as, "I have gangrene and wish for my infected leg to be amputated") and some of our desires are disordered (such as, "My body is healthy but I want my leg removed.").

Intentionally maiming a healthy part of one's body may be the desire for someone with BIID, but isn't this proof that not all human desires should be acted upon? Wouldn't we consider it medical malpractice for a physician to fulfill such a disordered desire?

Correspondingly, the fact that someone claims to want to die doesn't mean we should follow through, since the desire is a disordered one. We can label such a wish that way by considering human intuition (regardless of embracing a religious worldview or not) when it comes to life and death:

- In 2014, there was an outbreak in Africa of the deadly virus Ebola. What did people fear? Death. What was the world's response? Preserve life.

- That same year, a Malaysian airline plane was shot down and crashed over the Russia-Ukraine border, killing almost 300 people. One Scottish couple, Barry and Izzy Sim, as well as their baby, were supposed to be on that flight but due to overbooking were put on another plane. What do you think their reaction was to not being on the deadly trip? Gratitude at being *alive*.[82]

- Or imagine this thought experiment: You run into an elderly friend at the grocery store who announces her first grandchild was born. Wouldn't "Congratulations! How wonderful!" easily fall off your lips? What if shortly thereafter she lets you know her husband was diagnosed with cancer—wouldn't you just as quickly express sorrow and sadness? What does that tell us? We rejoice at life and are saddened by death (or the potential of death).

- Animal Planet TV aired a program called *I Shouldn't Be Alive*, which documented real stories of people who got stuck in avalanches, canyons, the ocean, etc., who almost died but they hung on. Captions for the series trailer were "Never Give Up" and "The Power to Protect" and "There is a strength within us all... The will to survive." It demonstrates the overpowering drive to choose life and not death. Just consider rescuers who search for missing people: there is joy and elation at finding people alive, and sadness and devastation when rescuers arrive too late.

These are just a few illustrations to show our human intuition of choosing life over death. Therefore, when someone says they want to be killed, we should not follow through because such a wish is disordered. If we dig deeper, we will likely see the disordered desire has beneath it an *ordered* one—perhaps a desire to no longer suffer or a desire to be with Jesus in Heaven. Those are good but killing is not; therefore, whatever action we take, we must ensure it is not that.

C. When the person dies, if I trace their death backwards to its cause, what will the cause be?

While recognizing that there comes a time for all of us to ultimately pass away, the key is that that time should not come at the hand of another or the self, but due to factors beyond our control, such as age, disability, or illness. So we can ask, has a person died due to a condition, or were they killed (whether by omission or commission) at the hands of another? If, for example, someone has cancer and is smothered to death by a pillow, it would not be accurate to say the individual died from cancer. Nor would it be accurate to say the individual "stopped breathing." Instead, they would have died from being killed by way of oxygen deprivation intentionally inflicted by another party with the purpose of ending their life. The same is true with a euthanasia injection or pill—in such cases the underlying disease is not what takes a person out, but rather killing at the hands of another (whether the patient requested it or not) is what ends their time on earth. This reality gives us an opportunity to think about how cold assisted suicide is, and how it lacks compassion—even though society tries to "dress it up" with compassionate appearances by throwing parties the night before or playing peaceful classical music while surrounding a loved one. At the end of the day, in such a situation the "moment of death" is calculated and pre-meditated, it is quite literally at the hand of one who should be a trusted beloved, rather than the consequence of illness.

D. Is a particular course of action proportionate or disproportionate?

Death *will* come for each of us. So how do we determine when it is death's time and when we should continue with treatment? This is where examining whether a treatment is proportionate (or ordinary) versus disproportionate (or extraordinary) is helpful. By looking at the totality of an individual's health condition and prognosis, the interventions we have available to us, and how a particular patient's body will respond, we should ask: Will a treatment offer a reasonable hope of benefit and not be excessively burdensome (proportionate) to the patient, or would it not offer a reasonable hope of benefit and be excessively burdensome (disproportionate)? There is a moral duty to pursue the former but not the latter.

For example, a friend of my friend had ovarian cancer that she battled for just over two years. Initially she pursued all kinds of treatment and medical interventions with the hopes of killing the disease invading her body. As time progressed, however, and the disease took on a life of its own, it became tragically clear that pursuing treatment would not ultimately eradicate the cancer. In fact, the aggressive interventions would bring a series of negative complications to her that would not be balanced by benefits. She reasonably ceased treatment that was clearly disproportionate in her case, and was given excellent hospice care until she passed away.

Or, I think of the time during one of my presentations where a plastic surgeon, who had several decades experience as a burn specialist, raised his hand during Q & A. He shared with the audience that some patients aren't saved. The reality is, there are times when a medical team ceases disproportionate interventions and a patient succumbs to the underlying condition. But, he cautioned, as a physician he rejects homicide. In no uncertain terms he pointed out that doctors should not kill a patient. There is a significant difference between killing someone versus not being able to ward off death.

So let's consider the concepts of proportionate and disproportionate interventions as they relate to a specific case, such as someone who has stopped breathing. Should CPR (cardiopulmonary resuscitation) be done? That depends.

Ethicist Rev. Tadeusz Pacholczyk provides this helpful information for discernment:

> Some of the possible burdens that may need to be considered in deciding whether to pursue resuscitative interventions for a patient would include some of the following: the risk of rib or other bone fractures, puncture of the lungs by a broken bone (or from the trauma of lung compression and decompression), bleeding in the center of the chest, cerebral dysfunction or permanent brain damage...
>
> During resuscitative efforts, elderly patients are more likely to experience complications or to have ribs break during CPR. Younger patients, on the other hand, tend to show a greater resilience and are often better able to tolerate CPR. Patients suffering from advanced cancer are also known to fare poorly following resuscitative efforts.[83]

So rather than make sweeping statements like, "You should always do CPR" or "You should never do CPR," decisions are made on a case-by-case basis. This way one can consider, in light of a specific patient's condition along with an intervention's benefits and risks, whether a procedure would be proportionate or disproportionate in that moment.

E. Are we talking about treatment or care?

Contrasting treatment versus care enables us to see that some human needs are so basic, they shouldn't be classified as "treatment" (something only those with specific conditions need) but, rather, "care" (something everyone needs).

Administering nutrition and hydration is an example of care, not treatment, because food and water are basic requirements for all humans to live. Absence of these can not only lead to death, but to great suffering until one dies (just consider your own experiences of hunger pain or thirst). The general rule should therefore be to administer these. Having said that, even care like food and water can become, for some people who are very sick and dying, disproportionate and it would be morally acceptable to cease administering these. Let's look at some specifics:

> [A] patient in the last stages of stomach cancer is already dying from that condition. Such a dying patient, or others who can speak for the patient, may decide to refuse further feeding because it causes pain and gives little benefit. The administration of nutrition and hydration in this case would pose a burden on the stomach cancer patient that is disproportionate to its benefit.[84]

Reverend Pacholczyk once again provides helpful insight on this topic:

> In some cases, feeding tubes may actually cause significant problems of their own for a patient. For example, if someone is facing an advanced illness, perhaps with partial bowel obstruction, a feeding tube can sometimes cause them to uncontrollably vomit when fed, offering little nutritional benefit, and raising the specter of lung infections and respiratory complications if they inhale their vomit. The feeding tube under these conditions may become disproportionate and unduly burdensome, and therefore non-obligatory.
>
> In some instances, providing drips and nasogastric feeding tubes can interfere with the natural course of dehydration in a way that causes acute discomfort to the patient facing imminent death.

Intravenous fluids also tend to increase respiratory secretions, making it more difficult for patients to catch their breath or causing them to cough. Extra fluids may result in a need to suction the patient's lungs. Providing IV hydration can also cause a flare up of fluid accumulation in the abdomen and expand the edema layer around tumors, aggravating symptoms, particularly pain. The use of IV drips and feeding tubes will always have to be evaluated in terms of the totality of the patient's condition, taking into account any undesirable effects, and the likelihood of benefit.[85]

Notice how the pro-life position on assisted suicide is consistently against killing while not being against dying. It accepts there comes a point where one will raise the white flag of surrender to the thief called death. Some interventions, even care, might not be pursued because they do not reasonably offer benefit and are excessively burdensome. Having said that, that is not always the case.

Consider the story of Terri Schiavo. She was a young American woman who, in 1990, collapsed at home and went several minutes without oxygen. As a result, she acquired a brain injury. She eventually came out of a coma but due to difficulty swallowing she required a feeding tube.[86] In this case, the feeding tube was not excessively burdensome for her body and it was showing a hope of benefit: her body was capable of processing nutrients. Terri even showed some cognitive progress the following year when she was able to speak some words at rehabilitation sessions.[87]

Her husband Michael had guardianship of Terri but he got into a relationship with another woman and had children with her all while Terri was in care. Furthermore, when Terri developed a urinary tract infection (UTI), which is simply cured by antibiotics, Michael denied such treatment.[88] A law overrode his wishes, but the fact that he wanted to stop proportionate treatment is alarming. Providing antibiotics in the presence of her UTI was not excessively burdensome and it had a hope of benefit.

To make a long story short, a legal battle ensued for years and ultimately Michael succeeded in having stopped what was, in Terri's case, proportionate care of nutrition and hydration. Terri's feeding tube was removed and she was even denied hydration or nutrition by mouth. It took almost two weeks of her suffering before she succumbed to death by severe dehydration.[89]

In this case, Terri did not have an underlying disease that was killing her. She didn't have, for example, end stage stomach cancer that could make receiving food burdensome. Instead, she was a woman who developed a disability and required help receiving the care of food and water. She didn't die from a disease; she died by intentional killing, by way of severe dehydration.

F. How does *The Principle of Double Effect* apply in a particular intervention?

Sometimes when people commit an action, that act produces effects, some of which are good and some of which are bad. How does one determine whether the original course of action may be ethically pursued? This is where *The Principle of Double Effect* is a helpful guide. The steps of this principle are as follows:

1. The action in itself must be good or indifferent. The action must not be intrinsically evil.
2. The good effect cannot be obtained through the bad effect (because then the end would justify the means).
3. There must be a proportion between the good and bad effects brought about (e.g. life against life); the foreseen beneficial effects must be equal to or greater than the foreseen harmful effects (the proportionate judgment).
4. The intention of the subject must be directed towards the good effect, and merely tolerate the bad effect.
5. Some say there is also a fifth requirement—that there does not exist another possibility or avenue.[90]

We can consider these steps in light of administering pain medication. What if doing so will have an effect of shortening a person's life? Would that be considered euthanasia/assisted suicide or is it ethical?

The action of administering pain medication when someone is in pain is a good, not an evil action, so it fulfills the first criteria. From that good action may flow two effects: The good effect is the alleviation of pain; the bad effect may be the shortening of the patient's life. The pain is alleviated, not by way of the other effect of shortening a patient's life, but by way of the direct action of administering pain meds. There is proportion between these effects, and the intention is directed toward the good effect. Of course, if there were pain medication that only had the good effect and not the bad, then that ought to be used. But in the absence of an alternative, it is not killing a person to administer pain killers; it is killing pain.

It is worth noting that when administering pain killers, only the amount necessary to actually alleviate the pain should be administered. If someone gives more pain killer than necessary (wrong action) with the intention of killing the patient (wrong intention), then that is immoral. But if someone gives the amount of pain killer necessary to alleviate pain (good action) with the intention of helping the patient (good intention), then that is moral.

It is also worth mentioning that although this example helps us understand *The Principle of Double Effect*, it doesn't follow that administering pain medication will necessarily shorten one's life. In fact, a friend of mine who is a palliative care physician told me, "There is good evidence that proper pain control actually lengthens life while controlling pain."

The point in all of this is to recognize death will come to us, but we should not play the grim reaper and be the dealer of death. Instead, we ought to alleviate suffering without eliminating the sufferer. A place where this is achieved is Calvary Hospital in New York, which is America's "only hospital dedicated to providing hospice and palliative care to adult patients with advanced cancer and other life-limiting illness."[91]

The hospital's executive medical director emeritus is Dr. Michael J. Brescia who transformed the world of medicine and ethics in two significant ways: 1) He co-invented the Brescia-Cimino Arterio-Venous Fistula, which helped 50,000 people in the first year and millions still today.[92] 2) He prioritized people over profits by releasing his invention immediately instead of handing it over to a drug company which would have delayed its release by a year (even though that patent would have made Dr. Brescia huge sums of money).[93]

In an interview he said the following:

> At Calvary, we have never, ever, in any way, hastened death purposely. We'll argue, 'We love you enough to never kill.' We come across a symptom that is unacceptable, and we treat the symptom until there is relief. Our doctrine is succor, compassion, love, gentleness.[94]

He also remarked, "At Calvary we treat 6,000 patients a year, and no one, after they have been here for 24 hours, asks for assisted suicide. No one: no matter what's wrong, and we've seen some terrible cases. Not when you reach out with arms of love."[95]

5

Human Dignity is Unconditional

"The greatest disease in the West today is not TB or leprosy; it is being unwanted, unloved, and uncared for. We can cure physical diseases with medicine, but the only cure for loneliness, despair, and hopelessness is love. There are many in the world who are dying for a piece of bread but there are many more dying for a little love."[96]

It was Lent several years ago when a 19-year-old old Canadian teenager set off on a pilgrimage to the Holy Land—well, that's how she described her plan to her friends.[97] But where she was going was not the traditional Holy Land of Israel where Christ once walked; instead, her Holy Land would take her to India where Christ still walked—in the suffering human souls she would serve. "We all have the desire to help somebody, to do something good," said Grace, one of my audience members, "but for me it was more that I wanted to meet Christ and have an encounter with him and I knew that's what Mother Teresa and her sisters found in the poor."

It was the most solemn day of the Christian calendar—Good Friday, the day where Christ-followers around the world remember the sacrifice of Jesus laying down His life on the cross. For the volunteers at the Missionaries of Charity's home for the dying, this is a day off to enter into prayer and reflection. Grace, however, felt compelled to ask for a special exception: Since the sisters had to serve the sick that day anyway, could she help them as long as she did so slowly and in a spirit of prayer? They said yes, providing an opportunity for Grace to enter deeply into the "Stations of the Cross" in a way more real than ever before.

When one reads of Christ's torture, we see how some close to him betrayed and abandoned him. But then there were the others—those like Simon of Cyrene and Mary His mother—who stood by His side and by their presence were a comfort. This was the example Grace knew she ought to follow. At one point she found herself kneeling beside the bed of a dying man, slowly and patiently administrating hydration through a dropper; it was then where the words of Christ played over in her mind: "I thirst" (John 19:28). As she was reminded of Christ dying on the cross with a crucifix on the wall, she knew she was also encountering Christ in the individual lying in the bed before her. While incapable of eliminating suffering, she did what she could to alleviate it.

These moments taught that loving glances, hand-holding, sitting with, and gentle patience can bring much peace to those who are suffering. As Grace remarked,

> Regardless of what life experiences a person has had before death, when they go through such great suffering it has a transformative power—when the person allows himself to be loved and cared for by others there's such a deep and beautiful reflection of God's love between the sufferer and the one who is suffering with.

Some people who arrived at Mother Teresa's home were extremely sick and expected to die, but with good care they were restored to health. Others, however, had their last breath—not on a dirty street ignored by passersby, but in a home surrounded by people caring for them. Grace told me that the few deaths she saw were incredibly peaceful: "I think it's because the patients knew they were loved."

She shared another story about a man who had a facial cancer and most of his face was distorted or missing as a result—his jaw was gone, even some of his neck, so that it was just his eyes, the bridge of his nose, and then the rest was bandaged off. "I had the honor of being able to be with him the last half an hour before he died," Grace shared (although she didn't know at the time he was so close to death). "I remember making eye contact with him across the room for the first time and then going to see him and greet him and that was the moment that bound my heart to Christ, and the dying, and the home for the dying." She didn't see the grotesqueness of what cancer had done to his face; instead, she told me that she peered deep into his eyes and was captivated by the beauty of his soul.

We prove that a sick, fragile human being has dignity by how we treat him. Grace explained how this was upheld at the home for the dying: she and the others would help patients brush their teeth, assist men with shaving, and brush women's hair. The fact that the individuals were dying did not mean such basic grooming should be withheld. Far from it, to do such simple acts was to stress the dignity of the person—to acknowledge that they were worth caring for regardless of their condition.

I've therefore been mystified by the notion of assisted suicide advocates that to be denied assisted suicide is to be denied a death with "dignity." The not-so-subtle implication is that if one dies naturally, entirely dependent on others to feed him, change him, or wipe his drool, that he has somehow lost his dignity.

Consider these words of a wife and mother named Liz who was struck with advanced incurable kidney cancer:

> The moment we label suicide an act of dignity, we've implied that people like me are undignified for not ending our lives; or worse, we're a costly burden for society. What a lonely, uncharitable, and fake world we live in if we think it's somehow undignified to let people see us suffer, to love us and care for us to the end.[98]

A simple dictionary definition of dignity is this: "the quality or state of being worthy, honored, or esteemed."[99] A sick person, a dying person, cannot lose her dignity because she *is*—in other words, by her existence she ought to be honored, respected, and cared for.

Consider that when something is valuable in and of itself we act differently around it—we treat it as its nature demands. Consider an expensive, one-of-a-kind painting: a museum curator is going to make sure the valuable artwork is handled with care. Or consider a sleeping newborn baby: parents will walk quietly and gently into the bedroom to check on the child, avoiding making startling noises. When a painting is covered with dust or a baby soils her diaper we do not say these have lost their dignity—rather, we respond in such a way as to acknowledge the dignity that lies within (by dusting the painting and changing the child).

So ought our response be to those who are dying—not hastening death, not eliminating the person, but instead being present and caring for the individual with the gentleness and reverence that their dignity inspires.

This perspective brings to mind a news story about a Parisian apartment being untouched for decades so that those who entered in 2010 seemed to walk back in time.[100] That year, its owner, Mrs. De Florian, passed away and the suite that she owned—but hadn't lived in for decades—was entered. It was a goldmine discovery of countless valuable antiques. Because it appeared to have been unlived in for 70 years, the interior was covered in a thick layer of dust and cobwebs. Amidst it all was a painting by Italian artist Giovanni Boldini that was subsequently auctioned for 1.8 million Euros.[101] Here's the point: That piece of art was considered valuable even though it was covered in dust. It did not lose its value just because dirt had landed on it. It did not lose its value just because it had not been admired for decades. It did not lose its value just because its existence had been unknown. Its worth was there all along, and discovering its existence was a reminder of that worth. Discovering its existence resulted in ***restoration***. Discovering its existence resulted in ***appreciation***. So it is with humans: When a person's dignity is covered by "dust" or hidden and unknown, our response should be to restore and appreciate, not reject the other as having "lost" their dignity.

Think about the meaning of the word love. In Greek there are at least four words to denote the different types of love: agape, eros, philia, and storge. Agape love indicates unconditional love. It is the most profound of all the loves because it involves knowing another's weaknesses, wounds, mistakes, sins, and brokenness and yet loving them in spite of it all. It is loving without conditions.

Like agape love, human dignity should similarly be viewed as unconditional. Because humans are made in God's image (Genesis 1:27), because it was after God made humans that He surveyed His creation and described it as "very good" (Genesis 1:31) instead of the previously-used word "good" that the rest of creation was described as, because God sent His only Son for the salvation of humans and not for other creatures (John 3:16), it follows that humans have dignity. Sin does not destroy our dignity; sin defaces our dignity. Even the actions of a mass murderer do not cause him to lose his dignity. Instead, his actions cause him to mar, to soil, or to betray his dignity.

Think about what happens when someone is sick and dying: there is much that seems to be a betrayal of her dignity—vomiting, soiling oneself, tumors, disfigurement, pain, fevers, and so forth. These things do not take away one's dignity but should prompt us to respond so as to affirm the dignity that is there but covered up. Assisting someone's suicide does not affirm their dignity; it disregards it. It feeds into the false idea that their dignity was lost when their health and abilities were lost. Tenderly caring for someone and improving their circumstances is what reaffirms, time and again, that they have dignity.

That is what makes the story of Martin Pistorius both terribly tragic and incredibly beautiful. I think the best place to begin is where Martin does in his book *Ghost Boy: The Miraculous Escape of a Misdiagnosed Boy Trapped Inside His Own Body*. He starts by referencing Barney, the purple dinosaur. We are all likely familiar with the childlike jingle Barney sang. And let's be honest—it's rather annoying to hear, especially again and again. So imagine being subjected to that song day in and day out. For years. Imagine hating it, but not being able to tell the people subjecting you to it that that's how you feel. Imagine not being able to communicate your disdain because you cannot speak.

Now imagine sitting in a wheelchair and being strapped in because you have lost control of your body and might fall out. Now imagine the strap is digging into you and it hurts. But imagine you cannot tell anyone that's what is happening because, again, you cannot communicate. So you are forced to sit in agony.

Or imagine it's time for a shower and your caregiver splashes cold water on you and gets soap in your eyes, as though you do not feel the terrible sting. But you do. And it hurts.

These are just a few of the examples of suffering Martin faced while he endured ten years of being "locked in"—a functioning mind trapped in a barely functioning body. It all began in the 1980s when he was growing up in South Africa and became sick at the age of 12. What appeared as the flu got progressively worse, so that Martin would sleep constantly and cease being able to talk. His muscles wasted and his limbs became spastic. His hands and feet curled in on themselves like claws. For the first few years of his illness he was not aware, but then something happened. Martin began to wake up. Except no one realized that. And for almost a decade he was a mind trapped in a body. His suffering, as I outlined above, doesn't even come close to other agonies he would face, such as torturous physical and sexual abuse at the hands of some of his caregivers.

Because Martin could no longer do what he once did, because he was regressing rather than progressing, because he appeared to be unaware, some people treated him like trash. Their actions showed they did not see unconditional dignity in him. Instead, dignity to them was *conditional*—and Martin simply did not reflect the right conditions.

From the perspective of unconditional dignity, however it doesn't matter if Martin was aware or not, it doesn't matter if he would get unlocked (as he eventually did) or not. What mattered was that he existed and should have been reverenced because of that.

Someone who had that correct perspective and who was also mightily *perceptive* would come along and make a discovery. Her discovery was not of Martin's dignity, for she already recognized that; instead, her discovery was of Martin's unleashed potential.

Virna was her name. And when I read about her in Martin's book, the beauty of her soul made me want to cry. Virna is the epitome of how we all should interact with another.

She was a caregiver who would use sweet-smelling essential oils to tenderly massage onto Martin's twisted body. She stood out because of her love.

Martin writes,

> Virna looked at me properly… She saw that my eyes really were the windows to my soul and became more and more convinced that I understood what she said.
>
> ***
>
> Others wash and wipe, dress and dust me down, but it's always as a means to an end. Only Virna touches me for no other reason than to soothe my aching body…[102]

Virna believed Martin did not have the mind of a 6-month old baby as doctors had said. She believed he should be sent for testing to see if he could communicate. She became an advocate for him, stressing to his parents how important it was to look into what his actual abilities were.

Thanks to Virna, Martin became unlocked. What has become of him today? He has regained the use of his upper body. He communicates via computer. He enters wheelchair races. He drives a car with his hands. He has given a *TED Talk*. He got married. And in 2018, he and his wife had a baby boy.[103]

How many people are alive today and mistreated like Martin once was? Rather than assisted suicide, we ought to affirm their dignity as Virna did Martin's. And we should remember, Virna treated Martin with tenderness **before** he got unlocked; her kindness was not because of what could be; it was because of who he was. Whether the sick and elderly in our midst "come out" of their lack of awareness or not, our job is to tenderly care for them. Our job is to be like Virna.

Just as people misunderstood Martin, some misunderstand God. In moments that are tough and painful, we can be tempted to get angry at God, wondering why He doesn't use His power in ways we would. Martin, however, trusted in God's loving presence and wisdom even when so much around him was confusing. Martin wrote,

> The one person I talked to was God... He was real to me, a presence inside and around that calmed and reassured me...I talked to Him endlessly because I knew we shared something important. I didn't have proof that He existed, but I believed in Him anyway because I knew He was real. God did the same for me. Unlike people, He didn't need proof that I existed—He knew I did.[104]

Having said that, what if some proponents of assisted suicide do not object to the main point of this chapter? What if they say they mean something different by "dignity" when they speak of "dying with dignity"? What if they mean someone should be able to "die without embarrassment," thus implying that reliance on others, particularly when one is very vulnerable and needing others for one's private care, is embarrassing? What if they aren't meaning to say that the person who rejects assisted suicide lacks dignity in her nature, but instead are meaning to say that the person who embraces assisted suicide wants dignity in the particular mode she uses to die?

Even with that perspective, there are problems. Going back to the aforementioned definition of dignity, one must ask, how does killing oneself lead to a state of being worthy, honored, or esteemed? Do we have a right to not be embarrassed? Even when we are embarrassed, does that give us license to do ***just anything*** to get out of the embarrassment? Do we really want to say embarrassment justifies killing? How does dying in weakness, pain, and reliance on others translate into a mode of death that lacks dignity? Simply put, it doesn't. In fact, it is moments of amplified weakness and fragility that draw compassion out of others that reinforce we are worthy of their attention, that we are to be honored by their care, and that we are to be held in high regard by them.

6

Human Flourishing Occurs in a Context of Connection

Who knew that expediting one's passport renewal could lead to dramatic, painful, and life-altering turns, but that was the experience for a British teenager back in 2009.

When Henry Fraser was just 17 years old, he scheduled a trip to go on vacation with some friends from school, travelling from his home of England to the beaches of Portugal. When he got in line to board the plane, an airline worker observed something Henry had not noticed: His passport was expired. While his friends continued their journey, Henry dejectedly returned home. His parents knew how much the trip meant to him and quickly put plans in motion to make it possible for Henry to achieve his dream. Little did any of them know that a seemingly simple and loving gesture would quickly turn a dream into a nightmare.[105]

After a 200-mile drive to a passport office, Henry found himself with an updated and expedited passport and on a new flight, landing in Portugal only 24 hour later than planned. After several days of fun in the sun, during a particularly hot moment on the beach, Henry ran into the ocean to cool off. But a seemingly fun and refreshing decision to dive into the water would lead to Henry's head colliding with the seabed, leaving him paralyzed from the shoulders down.[106]

In Henry's memoir about his trauma and triumph, about his suffering and survival, he shares inspiring insight about facing hardship. Although he would have to re-learn how to breathe, cough, and swallow, although he would continue to live without being able to move his arms or legs as before, ten years later Henry Fraser is not just surviving; he is thriving. What led to this human flourishing?

Although there are various factors, what is abundantly clear upon reading his book, *The Little Big Things: A Young Man's Belief that Every Day Can be a Good Day*, is the life-giving power of human connection. Henry's family stood by his side enabling him to know at the depths of his being, "...that I wasn't alone."[107] He wrote about his parents who spent so much time in his presence, doing activities with him like crosswords, or reading to him, or simply updating him about the lives of their loved ones outside the hospital.

He also wrote, "with the love of others, whoever they are, you can face darkness and look through to the other side."[108] When reflecting on his three brothers coming to his bedside, he said, "It was as if their tears and bear hugs were giving me a massive surge of life and I knew, in those moments, that with my brothers by my side, I would survive this."[109]

If being carried by others can help a paralyzed person move forward, what makes someone become stagnant?

That question is answered in the movie *A Man Called Ove*, based off of the novel by Fredrik Backman. This Swedish film with English subtitles tells the tale of a grumpy old man with no desire to live. In fact, in his isolation and misery, Ove tries, repeatedly, to kill himself. As it should happen, each time he comes close to succeeding, an unsuspecting neighbor calls on him for help. As the film progresses the viewer begins to understand why Ove is as he is. The unfolding backstory reveals what is under the surface. This allows one to see Ove with new eyes—to see his goodness and his pain and therefore to empathize with him.[110] As the heartwarming film unfolds, these key themes emerge:

1) Isolation and disconnection lead to despair. Ove is miserable not just because he has experienced profound suffering (after all, his neighbors also experience suffering but do not share his same misery). Ove is miserable because he is isolated.
2) Relationship can unlock the door to a person's heart.
3) When a person is needed *by* others, it teaches him he *needs* others (the reverse is also true).

Humans are made for relationship. How do we know this? First, we can look to the first creation story, when God said "Let us make man in our image, according to our likeness" (Genesis 1:26). God is a Trinity, three persons in one. God is a communion of persons between the Father, Son, and Holy Spirit, who are in a relationship of continually giving and receiving love. Humans, then, image God by being in a relationship of giving and receiving love. We can see that in the power humans have to create new life. The very beginning of the next generation is designed to come through a communion of persons. Whereas the circulatory system, respiratory system, or endocrine system is complete in an individual, the reproductive system is incomplete. Each individual has only half of that system. For it to work at its fullness, one needs the other half, which comes from another person. By God's designs, to *create* another human is to first *cleave* to another human, to create a communion of persons. Then, once new life is created, that life is nestled beneath the heart of the mother. Once again, we do not have life in isolation. We have new life who, by very design, needs another and is in communion with the mother. Love and life necessitate connection.

In the second creation story, when God created the world, amidst all the beauty of His creation, God looked at Adam and remarked, "It is not good for the man to be alone" (Genesis 2:18). It doesn't take much to see what happens when man is alone. We need only look to solitary confinement as a torture technique to see what happens when humans are removed from a communion of persons.

In the movie *Walk the Line*, based on the true story of musician Johnny Cash, there is a poignant scene where the characters of Johnny Cash and his first wife Vivian Liberto are fighting. The beginning of their marriage had involved poverty and work challenges, but as Johnny rose to fame, he also rose in wealth. That wealth, however, came with a price:

He was often away. As the two have a battle of words, Johnny looks at pregnant Vivian and lists all the things he got for her—a dream house, pretty things, and a car. He then demands, "What do you want from me?" Her answer? "I want you, John!!! I want you!"[111]

Where relationships are broken, humans experience profound suffering. Why? Because we are made for relationship—not things. And things are made for us—but not the other way around.

Consider filmmaker Roko Belic who once asked, "Why is it that people who have so little and have suffered so much seem to be happier than other people who are more fortunate?"[112] He presents the answer in his 2011 documentary, *Happy*. While there are various factors that contribute to our happiness, such as enjoying the beauty of nature, a key factor is satisfying relationships. The film shows that regardless of people being in poverty, aged, or living with disfigurement from a traumatic accident, we experience happiness when we have people to commune with.

That point was reinforced at an event similar to *TED Talks* that I spoke at in Puebla, Mexico. In 2019, when I was at *La Ciudad de las Ideas* (CDI) I listened to fellow presenter Tal Ben Shahar, a professor who teaches the most popular course at Harvard on positive psychology, which is all about happiness. He emphasized the point that relationships with people, rather than things, is a determining factor in happiness. He talked about a psychology experiment where people were given money and told to buy themselves something; following that, their mood/happiness was measured. Similarly, people were given money and told to donate it to someone/some cause; subsequently that group's happiness was measured. The latter group showed longer-lasting happiness than the former. He then used that point to reference something from his first language, which is Hebrew. He said that his favorite name is "Natan" which is a palindrome that means "to give" and his message was that when you give you receive (and that concept is reinforced in the fact that the name is spelled the same forward or backwards).

But, in order to give you need someone to give to—you need relationship. When children go to school, we often think about what adults can teach them. And yet, unknowingly, it is children that have the most profound lesson of all to teach adults: We need each other. Think about the utter vulnerability of a newborn baby who relies on someone to do everything for her. Consider 5-year-olds who, if left to their own devices, would probably eat cereal for every meal.

The need for children (and thus adults) to have strong relationships has led to a fascinating body of research related to attachment theory. In a book about the attachment styles of secure attachment, anxious attachment, and avoidant attachment, authors Amir Levine and Rachel Heller write about the importance of healthy, close, loving relationships. When writing about the pitfalls of the avoidant attachment style, they reference the book *Into the Wild*. They talk about its main character, Chris, who sought to live self-reliant. In his trek to the Alaskan wilderness, he met people who wanted him to be a part of their lives, but he rejected that. In his rugged individualism, he lived for months on his own until he died. Shortly before his passing, he wrote in his journal, "Happiness [is] only real when shared."[113]

What Chris learned the hard way is what children, by their very existence, teach us: we need relationship. And as the "circle of life" does a 360, we typically end as we began: Teaching the "doers" around us that we are made to "be" in relationship. The elderly, the frail, the sick—they, like children, become the next teachers of life's greatest lesson: "Be. Be with me. Be connected. And as I am who I am in all my vulnerability—in my need—that will unleash from you great love." In needing to be loved, the beloved teaches a lesson to the lover—not only is there joy in loving, but the lover needs to be loved in return. Only in relationship can we experience life's greatest lesson. But assisted suicide robs us of that because it eliminates the very person to be in relationship with.

In June 2018, *Maclean's Magazine* published an article titled, "Canada's loneliest people," with a troubling subtitle: "25 per cent of Canadian seniors live alone, but there lies a little-documented population within that demographic that live in acute isolation."[114] The article reports on people going weeks without connection with others, and in desperation calling 911.

The article discusses what are termed "elder orphans." It describes the fate of some older people living in populated areas who, due to their fragility, cannot leave their homes. They end up being completely isolated and even when food is brought to them through meal delivery programs, it is dropped off for them to eat alone.

The article goes on, "One patient, who still has children and no serious medical concerns, asked ...about medically assisted dying—'not actively suicidal but feels she doesn't have pleasure in her life anymore.'"[115]

This reality should cause us to pause and deeply consider the solution. People who are disconnected, isolated, and lonely are suffering and some of them are wanting assisted suicide. The solution, rather than introducing assisted suicide, is to introduce a better environment for a lonely person—an environment of relationship and connection—so that we eliminate the adjective "lonely" rather than the noun "person."

It is worth considering that throughout the Scriptures there are many references to God's concern for orphans and widows and His command that we share His concern:

Hosea 14:4 says, "...in you the orphan finds compassion."

James 1:27 says, "Religion that is pure and undefiled before God and the Father is this: to care for orphans and widows in their affliction..."

Isaiah 1:17 says, "[L]earn to do good. Make justice your aim: redress the wronged, hear the orphan's plea, defend the widow."

Psalm 82:3 says, "Defend the lowly and fatherless; render justice to the afflicted and needy."

Psalm 146:9 says, "The Lord...sustains the orphan and the widow."

John 14:18 says, "I will not leave you orphans."

Deuteronomy 10:17-18 says, "For the Lord, your God...executes justice for the orphan and the widow."

Exodus 22:21 says, "You shall not wrong any widow or orphan."

Although it may seem obvious, it is important to ask the question, "***Why*** are we commanded to care for, and not harm, orphans and widows? ***Why*** are they mentioned in particular? ***Why*** would God set them apart?" I think the answer lies in their neediness. Orphans and widows are disconnected from what (who, really) they need. Children wouldn't survive without people caring for them. In ancient times, women would not survive without the support and provision of husbands or families. The individuals that fit in the categories of orphan and widow are individuals whose very ability to live is in jeopardy. But the issue is more than material means. When one thinks of orphans and widows what comes to mind is "aloneness" and "loneliness." Rather than ignore, abandon, or eliminate them, we are called to uphold, give justice to, care, rescue, and defend them. And all of those duties involve connection; they involve being in relationship.

7
We Ought to Celebrate Being

When two people meet for the first time, almost immediately a common question is asked: "What do you do?" It's interesting how we humans gravitate towards our activity as the topic of conversation. Perhaps it's because we humans are capable of so much and ***do*** so many varied things. While our actions can be impressive, what if they aren't?

Many years ago I remember seeing a billboard advertisement by the Canadian Down Syndrome Society. It showed a picture of a little girl with Trisomy 21 alongside the caption, "Celebrate Being." I loved it! In a world that celebrates "doing," that celebrates accomplishment, worldly success, etc., we mustn't forget that there would be no doing if there were not first a being. Even if a being cannot do in the present moment, if the being still is, he should be celebrated. The danger that arises when we celebrate doing more than being is that our very identity can get caught up in our accomplishments so that when we can no longer do, we think we should no longer be.

That brings to mind the story of Dr. David Goodall. He had accomplished much in his long life—living to the age of 104. He was a scientist in ecology and botany, teaching at universities in several countries. He was a researcher and editor and outside of his profession enjoyed acting, performing on stage for decades. He even played tennis until he was 90 years old. He had married three times and had both children and grandchildren. But his death in 2018 was not due to illness;

rather, it was due to his own hand: He travelled from Australia to Switzerland where he was killed by assisted suicide.

As I researched his story, these details stood out to me:

- One of his daughters said, "He wasn't a very good husband. He was a very, very difficult man because he was so focused on the science."[116] She said her dad had never said I love you and only did so when she drew it out of him the day he committed assisted suicide.[117]

- Two years before the assisted suicide, the university where he worked as an honorary research associate considered him unfit to work on campus (even though it was an unpaid position).[118] He challenged this and won but was given an alternative workspace.

- The year after that, he fell at home and was helpless on the floor for two days before his cleaner found him.[119]

- His eyesight was declining and he had long given up his driver's license.

- In an interview he said, "At my age, I get up in the morning. I eat breakfast. And then I just sit until lunchtime. Then I have a bit of lunch and just sit. What's the use of that?"[120] He also said, *"I am not happy. I want to die."*[121]

- A week preceding the assisted suicide he visited family in France and "was full of life," the observing reporter said.[122] While there, David was surrounded by the beauty of the countryside and was with family. Asked what he liked about this place he had visited so often he remarked, "Well, it's mainly the people here."[123]

Dr. Goodall was undoubtedly experiencing much loss. And the pain of that shouldn't be minimized. The thought of him lying weak and alone on the floor for days is utterly terrible. Why did embracing death have to be the solution to his suffering? How is that the best we can do? What if, instead of assisted suicide, he no longer lived alone? What if there were more to his days than sitting between meals? What if that space was filled with companionship? What if university students signed up to visit him, listening to the wisdom he had to impart and sharing their experiences and lives with him? What if he spent more time in France with the family and animals and countryside that were so uplifting for him? What if, after a lifetime of "doing," his ongoing living was to learn—and teach others—the power of "being"?

In Washington State there is an award-winning Intergenerational Learning Center that blends childcare under the same roof as a living facility for elders. From infancy to 5 years old, young children are in an environment with older adults. The very old and very young are brought together to interact with each other, and whether the means for connection is activities, music, or dance, at the heart of it all is celebrating being. It is about being connected, being in relationship, being in the present moment, and it becomes life-giving to both parties.

In a PBS story about the program, Charlene Boyd, the administrator of Providence Mount St. Vincent (the living center for elders) said, "All of us have common needs to be recognized. All of us have common needs to be loved, and all of us have common needs to share life together."[124]

Being recognized. Loved. Sharing life with others. That is what Dr. Goodall *needed*. He understandably *wanted* to drive, *wanted* to act, *wanted* to see better, *wanted* to do all kinds of things his frail body could no longer do. But in reality, he didn't need those things. His needs, however, were legitimate; they were necessary for human flourishing: Recognition, love, and connection.

How can we be more intentional about meeting peoples' legitimate needs? My friend Kathleen comes to mind. She shared this experience from when she lived in Western Canada:

> Every Friday morning, I've been spending an hour playing *Scrabble* with a lovely 93-year-old lady at a local care home. It's my simple way of helping the elderly find joy in their daily life. I'm always praying for opportunities to talk to her about God, or to simply show her that she is loved. Today, that opportunity

came in full force.

After our game, she outright asked me, 'What do you think of doctor-assisted suicide?' and pointed to an article from the paper on the topic. I told her that I felt it was very sad that anyone should feel the need to take their life, and it's our failure as a society when anyone is left feeling this way. After some time discussing this, she expressed to me that she can sympathize with people who don't feel they have a reason to live in their suffering, as she, too, often wonders why God still has her 'stuck in this wheelchair.'

With tears in my eyes, I was able to tell her what a joy she is to me, and that I look forward to visiting her every week. She teared up as well, shock in her eyes, and said, 'Really? Is that true?' I nodded, unable to get more words out. 'Well then, perhaps there is reason enough for me to be here.'[125]

Or take another friend of mine, a nursing student. She saw on a patient's chart that the patient had made an inquiry about euthanasia. My friend intentionally visited that patient more than others. Rather than discuss euthanasia, she spent time getting to know the woman. She became interested in her life; she connected over common interests and common backgrounds; she smiled and was joyful; she engaged the patient in conversation. In short, she poured love out on her. A few weeks later when my friend checked the patient's record, there was a note indicating the patient was no longer interested in euthanasia.

Connection holds great power, as my friends' stories prove, and intergenerational interactions can reinforce this. A few years ago, as my family gathered to celebrate my mom's 75th birthday, I sat at the table cuddling the latest addition to our family: my 3-month old nephew.[126] As I cradled Carl, my mind wandered, prompted by the increasing temperature of the blanket on my lap that swaddled his body: "Did he pee through his diaper?" I wondered. "Or is that just warmth from body heat?" Thankfully it was the latter, but it caused my mind to reflect on the total dependency of Carl on other people. And then my mind wandered to the elderly, some of whom are just as dependent on others as babies are. And with society's increasing acceptance of euthanasia, a thought came to mind:

"What if the world treated Carl like it sometimes treats the elderly?"

Would we leave him in his crib alone all day, turn the TV on for distraction but otherwise have minimal interaction with him? Would we scurry about to do lots of things but never take time to simply be with him? Would we possibly consider ending his life because, "What's the point anyways? He can't do much."

Now some might say that Carl, as opposed to an individual at the end of her life, will one day be a "contributing" member to society, and his is a life we shouldn't end. In other words, we would preserve Carl's life for what might be, but we would end an old person's life for what is no more. But what if Carl never matured enough to do what most adults do? What if he only lived for the next 6 months—knowing that, would we kill him now or would we savor and celebrate the little time we have left?

And so, as I thought further, it occurred to me that our world would be a better place if we asked a different question: "What if we treated the elderly the way we treat Carl?"

If that were the case, we would sing and play music. We would smile, laugh, and engage. We would soothe during seasons of sadness. We would hug. We would look at the other and simply delight in them.

As I have watched my four other nieces and nephews interact with their littlest brother, I've noticed something: When vulnerable, needy people are in our midst, it can bring out the softer, gentler, more caring sides of us.

I think about my strong-willed nephew who demonstrated such reverence for his little brother, delighting in holding him and sweetly kissing his cheeks. I think about my other nephew, a very sensitive child, who held his crying baby brother and repeatedly said "shh-shh-shh" until he had shh-ed him to sleep just like he observed his mom had done.

I think of my niece who loves to sing, dance, and be loud but who, when I arrived one day, crawled out from under the kitchen table and said

"Boo" in the quietest of whispers because Carl was nearby sleeping. I think of my then-9-year-old niece who's like a second mother, carrying her baby brother around like a doll and who is so good at comforting him.

Far from being a burden, the presence of Carl draws virtue out of the whole family. His need becomes an opportunity for our kindness. The same is true of the elderly—if only we let that be the case.

Many years ago, my sister texted me a story from her evening: She was trying to put her then-youngest baby, my niece Cecilia, to sleep and promised her oldest daughter, Monica, that she would come to her room later and read to her. But it took so long to put Cecilia down that by the time she got to Monica's room my eldest niece had fallen asleep—with the unread book in her limp hand. My sister texted me a photo explaining what happened with the caption, "MOM GUILT!" So I texted back, "You've given Monica something better than a bedtime story—you've given her a sister." She excitedly responded, "RIGHT! Perspective! Perspective! It's all about perspective!"

I realize not everyone can give their child a sibling, but everyone can give their child, and themselves, encounters with others, be it the elderly or someone else. That doesn't mean such encounters are always easy in the moment; after all, consider the stories from Chapter 1 of people who faced great suffering and challenges. The point here is that perspective is a powerful ally, and it is perspective which teaches us that encounters with the other can become moments to celebrate being in the human experience of love.

What are some specifics on how to celebrate being and thus make life richer? In our world filled with noise, sitting in silence can be like water to cracked soil. When we are quiet, we can more readily hear the still, small voice of God (1 Kings 19:12).

In the book, *The Power of Silence: Against the Dictatorship of Noise*, author Robert Cardinal Sarah says,

> Silence is difficult, but it enables man to let himself be led by God. From silence is born silence. Through God the silent, we

can gain access to silence. And man is unceasingly surprised by the light that pours forth then.

***

Silence is a quest and a form of charity, in which God's eyes become our eyes and God's heart is grafted onto our heart.[127]

The person who can no longer speak can celebrate being a teacher of the power of silence (although it is important we still help them find alternative ways to communicate so their needs are met). They become listener. Hearer of hearts. Secret keeper. They listen without interruption. Their gift is to receive.

Besides sacred silence, there are other ways we can celebrate being: Have you ever just sat, closed your eyes, and experienced the closeness of another holding your hand? Or have you done nothing except listen to a beautiful symphony with someone you care about? What about remembering being a child and having a story read to you? Or reading a story to a child? Or have you ever parked your car and watched the sun set over mountains? Or the ocean? And shared in that experience with another? Have you sat for a really long time at the beach, toes curled into the sand, feeling the descent of dusk lifting your spirits and triggering deep conversation? Have you found a sunny spot and let the heat of the sun warm your face and delight in the simplicity of that?

Have you been around people who are laughing and begun laughing too? Have you watched children perform a goofy play or a song that they made up and observed how they are immersed in delight? Have you held in your arms a sleeping newborn baby and been captivated and content just to stare like at a fireplace in winter? Have you sat and simply smelled freshly baked cookies and then savored the taste with the baker?

I remember meeting a couple who told me their relative would often bake cookies at midnight when her older children came home from being out with friends. She knew the delightful smell would entice them to the kitchen, providing an opportunity for a fruitful encounter with her children. It was so positive in maintaining a good relationship, that she expanded her approach to a street outreach program—getting a storefront and baking cookies when young people came out of bars in order to provide an alcohol-free environment with intentional opportunities for being in relationship with young people who often didn't have families to go home to.

This, and the other examples, are powerful moments of being that we can create for others, and share in with them.

8

Some of the Best Things in Life Come When We Release Control

At a presentation I gave on assisted suicide, an audience member raised her hand and shared that a few months prior, her aunt had opted for assisted suicide. She shared that the aunt had been surrounded by her family and was well loved. She described the orchestrated death as "beautiful." She said her aunt had methodically gone through a bucket list, had fulfilled all of her dreams, and was full and satisfied by the life she had lived. She was even leaving a significant financial legacy to help with cancer research. In the aunt's mind, her life was done, so she opted for suicide assistance.

I asked the audience member if she felt comfortable sharing more about her aunt's situation and condition. Since she was, the conversation continued in front of the crowd. I asked her what the aunt was dying from and what her health status was like before the assisted suicide. The woman shared that her aunt had cancer that had metastasized (spread to other parts of her body). She had a very bad heart. The more the woman described, the more it sounded to me like the patient would have been very near natural death. So I asked her if assisted suicide hadn't happened, how close to death she thought her aunt was—possibly weeks or even days? The audience member, who had a medical background, indicated it probably would have been mere days. So I asked, "Then why do assisted suicide? If she was literally days away from death anyways, why not give her comfort and surround her with family and friends until she passes naturally?"

The audience member didn't have much of a response other than to indicate it was what the patient wanted. Situations like this reveal a serious challenge we are up against: Desire for total control.

In 2014, the movie *The Giver* was released, which is based on Lois Lowry's book of the same name. It is a profoundly insightful dystopian story about a community that is built around "sameness." In this futuristic world people no longer know loss, death, hatred, or violence. But the trade-off? They also no longer know love, empathy, compassion, and joy. They are numbed by daily injections which rob them of emotions, the depths of the human experience. They wear clothes, but there is no fashion. They have dwellings, but not homes. They can see, but only in grey rather than color. In effect, they are like robots. In the quest to avoid suffering they have also avoided truly living. If they were able to feel deep affection and connection to another, then they would correspondingly feel the pain that comes when such a connection is severed. And so, every single aspect of society was meticulously controlled in order to avoid suffering.

It is perhaps an extreme example (definitely worth watching and/or reading) but it nonetheless demonstrates how control can go too far. Our society, particularly North America, is obsessed with control (and I can perhaps recognize this so readily because I'm someone who struggles with her own inordinate desire for control at times). But as *The Giver* reveals, trying to control everything comes with a cost. Are we willing to pay the price?

At the same talk where an audience member told me her aunt chose assisted suicide, another audience member remarked that if someone only has a few days left, rather than my approach of using that limited time to justify hanging on, his approach was to use the limited time to justify assisted suicide. *Nothing's going to happen in the days left*, he surmised, *so what's the point?*

First off, as addressed earlier in this book, if we allow assisted suicide for the reason of closeness to death, it is entirely arbitrary. How does one determine what is justifiable "closeness"?

Second, the legacy such an individual leaves behind for loved ones (and anyone who knows about the suicide assistance) is that when a person decides they've had enough, it is perfectly acceptable to end it all. Is that really the message we want to teach the next generation which is increasingly facing a suicide epidemic?

Most fundamentally, we simply can*not* know that "nothing" is going to happen in the days left. We do not know how those days will unfold. We humans are not omnipotent; we are not fortune tellers. And whether someone supports suicide assistance or opposes it, on that fact we should agree.

We can plan and control as much as we want, but we absolutely do not know exactly what the future holds—even if that future is short. Consider a 5-year-plan: People are encouraged to identify goals to aspire towards, but planning only gets us so far. How often have people looked *back* on a 5-year-plan and observed how differently it unfolded than expected? Moreover, when we plan and control too much we may create a future that is not as good as one built on surrender (consider that there's a reason the word "freak" is often attached to the word control, and a reason why a therapist will highlight the pitfalls of inordinate control in relationships).

When we are obsessed with control, we act as though we know best, and that what we have planned is exactly how things should be.

How many times have we been *wrong*?

How many times have we been *surprised*?

How many times have we been *grateful* things did not work out as we expected or even wanted?

What if another patient was to be impacted by the patient near death? What if long-suffering endurance, peaceful surrender, and loving community were to be lessons demonstrated to health care workers? What if the dying person was to have an epiphany about some regret in their past that they had been completely blind to? What if a patient in a semi-conscious state, who couldn't communicate, was, by their need and utter vulnerability, going to teach the people around them the merits of **being**, of loving, and of tenderness? What if this would only happen over the time period of natural death, and these would be missed opportunities if suicide assistance were chosen? The possibilities are endless, but the point is this: the possibilities exist, if we allow them to unfold.

So what if, when death comes knocking, we didn't answer? What if this wasn't denial or running away, but was simple acceptance? What if letting go of control meant letting death open the door itself without knowing the moment precisely? What if this, almost unbearable, waiting was for us to learn—at our end—what was man's downfall "in the beginning"; namely, that we humans are not in control, but God is? What if waiting for death to open the door was to teach us to not be afraid of letting go of control? What if it was to teach us that being led by a trustworthy source is better than leading when you actually aren't omnipotent? What if it was to give us a newfound freedom we didn't think possible with our limited perspective?

Some might object and say there is no God; they may claim there is no higher power to surrender to. Although it is true ***they believe*** there is no higher power to surrender to, it doesn't follow there is no god in such a person's world. On the contrary, the person who doesn't surrender to a higher power ***does*** have a god in their life: That god is themselves, insofar as it is themselves they hold as the final authority. But what if the self is a bad god? Since we know, without a doubt, that the self is prone to mistakes, error, vice, and has limited knowledge, isn't it risky to put one's trust on such shaky ground?

Consider the following: Anyone who has purchased IKEA furniture knows all about assembling it. The manufacturer provides a simple image of how to put together the various parts; if the instructions are followed, you'll get a Poang chair to sit on or a bookshelf for your literature collection. Do we take offence that IKEA's designers tell the buyer what to do? Of course not, because IKEA has the buyer's best interests in mind; it wants happy customers who return. IKEA created the furniture and knows how it will most aesthetically, functionally, and safely live up to its designs. IKEA's "rules for assembly" are not meant to unfairly restrict us, deny us, or control us. They are meant to free us. So it is with surrendering our control into the hands of an all-powerful God who loved us so much He lowered Himself, entered into the human experience, and then suffered and was killed in our place so we could spend eternity with Him in the ecstasy of Heaven.

Of course God gave us freedom to make decisions, but there is a significant difference between what we *can* do and what we *ought* to do. We *can* do anything, but we *ought* to do the right thing, that which was designed for our good. In big decisions and small, what is the thing we ought to do? That takes discernment. Even with surrender, we still have to make decisions (like the guidelines given in Chapter 4 on proportionate versus disproportionate actions). Therefore, I would suggest there is a balancing act with control—taking action, even directing how you think things should be, while having a flexibility to work with things as they arise. It's about rejecting rigidity. It's about seeing the merits of applying some control without becoming a control freak.

Let me give an example of this dance I am proposing: Have you ever written down your dreams? If so, have you then, years later, read old journals and discovered what you once envisioned actually came to fruition as you had transcribed? I have, and each time I made these revelations (there have been several), I was in awe of how what I hoped for came to be. But here's the thing: In some cases I had even forgotten I had had the dream, let alone written it down. So although in some ways I had made choices that influenced certain outcomes, there were so many factors I wasn't in control of that nonetheless occurred, unfolded, and contributed to the fulfilment of desire. Had I clung too tightly, had I tried too hard, had I been fixated on my timeline, with my limited knowledge, perhaps the dreams, as they did unfold, would not have. So there must be some give and take between acting and simply receiving, between directing and allowing for unfolding. It's like a dance, there's push and pull, give and take, leading and following. In a sense, dying naturally is the balance of these—it embraces life while accepting death will come. It tries interventions, and then accepts when these are futile. It acknowledges when death is approaching while at the same time it doesn't run to death. And it is in that space between living and dying, in that waiting, where there is room for the unfolding of things in a way we could not know, imagine, or orchestrate. Assisted suicide, and other ways of total control and manipulation, rob the individual and society of the greatness, and the gift, of the unknown.

This dance of the push and pull of control remind me of two people who suffered brutally, and differently: Brittany Maynard and Mattie Stepanek. The former's example is not to be followed whereas the latter's is.

Brittany died by suicide assistance at the age of 29. She had terminal brain cancer and wanted to end her life **before** the predicted end-stage consequences of this terrible malady would come to fruition. When she did pass away, she wrote in advance on Facebook, "Today is the day *I have chosen* to pass away... [emphasis added]."[128]

Watching an interview with Brittany's husband Dan on the *Megyn Kelly TODAY* show is certainly heartbreaking. What Brittany had endured, and what she feared would only get worse, are terrible realities for anyone to face. The way her husband framed things was the following: He said that if she hadn't chosen her controlled "gentle" death, she would have been "struggling and in pain."[129] He said her situation was already such that morphine wasn't adequately eliminating her pain. She faced brutal insomnia. There was nausea and vomiting. And as bad as that was, there were the seizures. He said that with grand mal seizures she would bleed out of her mouth because she'd bite through her tongue. She feared blindness and paralysis which were likely what would come with the growing tumor.[130] That's not what Brittany wanted the experience of death to be like. Understandably, no one would *want* that. And opponents of what she chose are not saying that if her death were that way it would have been a pleasant thing.

Opponents of suicide assistance would believe in working valiantly to alleviate the suffering of someone like Brittany. There are several strategies for pain control besides the morphine her husband said wasn't sufficient. These include more potent opioids, opioid adjuncts, nerve blocks, and so forth. Palliative care as a discipline has evolved markedly since its early days, and as a physician I know told me, practitioners can control pain in over 95% of cases. And so, opponents of suicide assistance are making the simple, but hard to accept, point that ending your own life should not be the solution no matter how terrible the circumstances.

When we release control, even when control is a means to avoid that which we fear, unexpected—even amazing—things can happen. And Mattie Stepanek is proof of that.

Mattie graced our earth for 13 short years, but his rich, supernatural legacy is far more than most leave in a long lifetime.

Mattie's beginnings were almost his end. He was diagnosed with an extremely rare form of muscular dystrophy called dysautonomic mitochondrial myopathy and it was predicted he would live for only hours after birth. But he defied the odds by living for more than a decade. His three older siblings, Katie, Stevie, and Jamie had shorter fates, dying at the ages of 20 months, 6 months, and almost 4 years old respectively; they were also burdened by this brutal disease—but that wasn't discovered until after Mattie's birth. When a label was finally given for what the children had, the doctors uncovered that, unknowingly, their mother Jeni had been the genetic carrier of the condition, and that she herself would be invaded by an adult onset version of it. Mattie and his mother not only suffered the loss of three siblings/children, they lived through seasons of profound poverty, relying on handouts. Little can be found online about Mattie's dad, but in an interview where Mattie was asked about him, the little boy simply said, "We're divorced from my father because he did some mean and scary things to us and I don't like to point fingers or talk about him." When the interviewer said, "You don't see him?" Mattie simply said, "No."[131]

Hospital stays and pain were a normal part of Mattie's life. He used a ventilator and a wheelchair. That is now his mother's fate. It gets worse: She was also diagnosed with cancer after Mattie died. If there were to be a case study in profound suffering, the Stepanek's would be a prime example. And yet, what they're known and admired for is mind-blowing resilience, other-worldly wisdom, and interminable hope.

When I first learned about this precious boy while writing this book, I was so inspired I became hungry to discover as much as I could about him. Watching interviews of him left me wondering, "Was he even human? How could a young child speak such profound insights? Did an angel take on bodily form and present as Mattie Stepanek?" I recommend watching the full-length interview of him on *Larry King Live* at the age of 11 to see why I ask what I do.[132]

Starting at age 3, Mattie began composing poetry, which his mother transcribed until he could write himself. He eventually published seven books. Millions came to know and love Mattie Stepanek. But here's the key—Mattie and his Divinely-inspired insights only became known throughout the world ***after*** he was on the brink of death. In 2001, when Mattie was on the cusp of turning 11, doctors were convinced he was weeks or even days away from dying. He had slipped into several comas and was bleeding out of his fingers, his lips, his trachea, and his feet.[133]

Mattie wanted to go home but the doctors did not want that because they said that dying there would not enable them to provide pain management like they could if he stayed at the hospital. They were concerned that if he went home his death would be agony.[134]

It is that type of death many fear. It is that type of death some would want to avoid by way of assisted suicide. It is that type of death that, as it seemed to be so rapidly approaching, some might declare, "What is the ***point*** of carrying on? What good could possibly happen? Let me just take control and make death happen now."

But what happened is that Mattie Stepanek prayed. What happened is that the bleeding stopped. What happened is that a miracle occurred. What happened is that the last three ***years*** of Mattie's life were just about to begin. What happened is that during that time period, his poetry, which he named *Heartsongs*, would be published. What happened is that his books would become *New York Times* bestsellers. What happened is that he would befriend former US president Jimmy Carter and he would appear on Oprah Winfrey's show several times, befriending her as well. What happened is that the world would come to know this tiny, fragile little sage named Mattie Stepanek because, as he said to his mother, "I have to live until the moment I die."[135]

We must never assume we know the future. We must never assume it's always best when we take control. Sometimes the most incredible things unfold when we release our grasping fingers, and surrender to what may be.

When Mattie eventually did succumb to his illness, Jimmy Carter gave the eulogy at his funeral saying, "We have known kings and queens, and we've known presidents and prime ministers, but the most extraordinary person whom I have ever known in my life is Mattie Stepanek."[136]

Oprah mentioned the thousands upon thousands of shows she's done, interviewing so many people, and she said, "Mattie would be the single biggest relationship that ever developed out of a show."[137] She described him as "One of the sweetest souls I have ever known."[138]

And of her son, Jeni Stepanek said, "He seemed to know God rather than learn about God. God was always his friend. God walked with him. One of the most profound things he said to me...as he got closer to death and he knew he was dying even before I could accept that, he said, 'Even the silence of God gives me strength.'"[139]

In an interview with Raymond Arroyo, Jeni recounts a story of Mattie hearing a nearby baby crying while Mattie himself was dying in the ICU:

> It's within a week of his death and he starts calling out, 'Nurse, nurse!' And his nurse came running in the room, 'What is it? What is it?' 'Cause this is a child who could not speak above a whisper, because he was gasping for breath. And when she came in, ready to console him, [to] meet his dying needs, [Mattie] said, 'Comfort the baby. The baby is crying. The baby is the future. Love the baby, 'cause that's how life goes on.' And the nurse just started crying and she went over and she picked up the baby and she said, 'Look Mattie, look, I'm loving the future. I'm holding the future for you.' And... his body was broken, broken, bones broken, gasping, and he still was concerned about others."[140]

Mattie did not take control of his death; instead, he chose to fully live a life of love until death came. His experience reminds me of the words of John O'Leary (whose story is told in the next chapter): "The most meaningful and truly best of life often occurs when we have the courage and humility to say yes to life, however it unfolds. It's only then we can be present for the people who need us most... and who we most need, too."[141]

Those words are what make Mattie Stepanek's witness so beautiful, and what makes Brittany Maynard's so tragic. Even when the unfolding of life can be scary or filled with suffering, there lies a great potency within those very same moments for beauty, transformation, inspiration, and love—if we let go of control and surrender.

In fact, isn't that what Jesus teaches us in the Garden of Gethsemane? Shortly before Jesus was arrested, He went to that garden to pray. Mark 14:33 says He "began to be troubled and distressed." Luke 22:44 records that Jesus "was in such agony and he prayed so fervently that his sweat became like drops of blood falling on the ground." In Mark 14:34 Jesus said to Peter, James, and John, "My soul is sorrowful even to death."

Then He cried out to His heavenly father, "Abba, Father, all things are possible to you. Take this cup away from me, but not what I will but what you will" (Mark 14:36). The book of Matthew records that Jesus expressed this prayer of surrender to the Father's will three times. Did Jesus face the utter brutality of crucifixion? Indeed, but He also experienced the resurrection and, in doing so, opened the gates to eternal life.

The surrender of "Thy will be done" is something psychiatrist Dr. Elisabeth Kubler-Ross draws on in her book *Life Lessons: Two Experts on Death and Dying Teach Us About the Mysteries of Life and Living*. She writes,

> Many of us labor under the illusion that control is always good, that it would be dangerous to just let the universe take care of things. But is our control really necessary to the workings of the world? We don't have to wake up early every morning to remind the universe to make the sun rise; when we turn our backs on the

ocean, the universe doesn't mess up and make the tide go the wrong way…

***

To surrender we simply rise every day and say 'thy will,' not 'my will.'[142]

9

Not all Choices are Equal, but They Create a Ripple Effect Either Way

In 1963, Rev. Martin Luther King, Jr., composed his *Letter from a Birmingham Jail* in which he wrote, "We are caught in an inescapable network of mutuality, tied in a single garment of destiny. Whatever affects one directly, affects all indirectly."[143]

Choices we make, big or small, positive or negative—these have a permeating influence.[144] They don't just affect us. Like a drop of food coloring in a glass of water, they diffuse into the surrounding area and impact people who, upon being touched, make other choices that in turn affect others.

The interconnectedness of our choices to other peoples' lives can be seen in a delightfully simple illustration: In 2013 in Newington, Connecticut, a customer at a coffee shop decided to pay the order of the patron behind him. That led to a chain reaction so that the next **one thousand customers** paid for the order of the person behind them.[145]

How true it is that we are "caught in an inescapable network of mutuality, tied in a single garment of destiny. Whatever affects one directly, affects all indirectly."

Or consider Zuly Sanguino, a Colombian woman who has faced profound suffering: She was born with no legs and only a portion of arms. Her father committed suicide when she was two. She was a victim of rape. She was bullied as a child and came close to suicide in her teenage years. Now, however, she is an artist and motivational speaker who lives an incredibly full and rewarding life, sharing messages that help others.[146]

She said, "One boy was about to take his own life with a gun when he saw a TV show I was on. He… decided not to take his life. He wrote to me and we're now really good friends."[147]

How many peoples' lives are better because of Zuly's witness? Correspondingly, had she committed suicide (on her own or with assistance) how many peoples' lives would be worse (and even over) because of her absence from this world?

How true it is that we are interconnected. Our choices impact people for better—or for worse. Consider the story of Will, a young man who was killed via the death penalty. His lawyer, David Dow, recounts Will's story in a *TED Talk*: Will's dad left his mom while she was pregnant with Will. Will's mom, afflicted with paranoid schizophrenia, tried to kill Will with a butcher knife when he was 5 years old. Will was taken into the care of his brother until that brother committed suicide. By age 9, Will was living on his own. He eventually joined a gang and committed murder.[148]

The choices of Will's father, mother, and brother undoubtedly impacted Will. There is simply no denying that we are "caught in an inescapable network of mutuality, tied in a single garment of destiny. Whatever affects one directly, affects all indirectly."

The next time someone supports assisted suicide because they "have a right to autonomy" and "should be able to do what they want because such a choice only affects the people who want to die," the above stories demonstrate that that simply isn't true. As poet John Donne once declared, "No man is an island."

Involving medical professionals in Person A's assisted suicide means Person B may no longer trust a health care professional to properly care for her life. Person A's assisted suicide will impact the disposition of the individual who supplies the life-ending drugs or injects the deadly poison, because you simply cannot kill another human being without that leaving a mark on your mind, your emotions, and your interactions with others. Person A's legally endorsed assisted suicide will create a climate where Person B may ask for assisted suicide too—not because she truly wants it, but, as mentioned previously, because she feels "guilted" into it by a culture that embraces it and makes her feel like a useless burden. Person A's assisted suicide may influence others to respond to their own suffering and obstacles by giving up instead of turning them into opportunities (as Zuly did). How do I know this? Because, to quote John Donne again, "No man is an island."

Indeed, my friend Kevin Dunn demonstrates this in two documentaries he directed: *Fatal Flaws* and *The Euthanasia Deception* (DunnMedia/Euthanasia Prevention Coalition). In these, he shows the slippery slope that is created when assisted suicide laws are introduced. He shares stories of patients being asked by physicians if they want to die, of criteria expanding from being terminally ill to those who are simply elderly, disabled or even depressed. He looks at countries like Belgium where a man's grandfather had a "hastened" death that he did not request, and of another man's mother who had depression and was euthanized without the son knowing. He cites a case of a family caring for their child with special needs, and how a society that has embraced euthanasia for over a decade has formed people in an ideology that prompts complete strangers to ask the family why they do not euthanize their child. We are interconnected, and one person's assisted suicide should not be viewed in isolation but seen as having a ripple effect on the rest of society. Just because we have an ability to do something, does not mean we have a right to do it.

In a conversation with a physician friend, I made the point that doctors are not baristas. Imagine going to a cafe to order a green tea and the barista telling you that you must have a latte. Maybe you're pregnant and the thought of anything with espresso makes you feel nauseous. Maybe you're allergic to the milk options available. Maybe you don't like creamy drinks. Maybe you're craving green tea. Whatever your motivation, the barista's job is to offer you a selection of choices but not dictate what you must have. The barista asks no questions about you—he simply takes your order.

Medical decisions are different. Physicians are trained *for years* to know the human body, its systems, pathologies that can develop, and interventions that heal. Sure, patients can take advantage of the World Wide Web and do their own research, but that is no replacement for years of formal education and clinical experience. Patients inform doctors of their symptoms and experiences so that physicians can put that through the filter of their wealth of knowledge, experience, and training. The doctor may believe multiple approaches are equivalent, and explain the pros and cons of those to the patient, but the doctor objectively has more credibility to provide a robust analysis of the situation than the patient does. This does not mean doctors are gods, nor does it mean they can never be wrong. It also does not mean patients are stupid. It just means that if someone knows more, they, simply put—***know more.***

So doctors should only recommend that which is medically indicated and in a patient's best interest. Patients should not demand things that are not medically indicated and not in their best interests. Further, the choices we do make should not be viewed in isolation. Positive choices will lead to a positive ripple effect and negative choices will lead to a negative ripple effect.

Consider the problem of copycat suicides. When actor Robin Williams committed suicide in 2014, it was reported there was an increase in suicides in the subsequent five months, particularly among men.[149] This isn't a new phenomenon.

Committing suicide after another person does is a phenomenon that goes back at least to a 1774 novel, *The Sorrows of Young Werther* by Johann Wolfgang von Goethe. The character in the book, Werther, commits suicide, and it has been argued that that led to a rash of suicides from some of its readers.[150]

In 2018, the World Health Organization published a document called *National Suicide Prevention Strategies*. In it they acknowledge the role that one person's suicide can have in leading others to act that way. In working to prevent such copycat behavior, they write,

> Responsible reporting by the media is an essential component of suicide prevention. Media professionals should not only refrain from the glamorized presentation of cases of suicide and thereby avoid imitation by vulnerable people, but should also communicate stories of someone coping successfully, seeking and receiving help.[151]

If suicide can lead to more suicide, we shouldn't be surprised that *assisted* suicide would lead to more assisted suicide. That is why we should not minimize the impact of our choices, and instead focus on creating positive ripple effects rather than negative ones.

Our interconnectedness and the power of positive influence is evident in the story of John O'Leary. When John was just 9 years old, 100% of his body was burned in a house fire. More than 80% of those burns were third degree. His chance of survival was less than half a percent. And yet, today he is married, a father to four children, a motivational speaker, and an author. He not only survived, he is thriving. In his book, *On Fire: The 7 Choices to Ignite a Radically Inspired Life*, John writes about the key factors that influenced how he arrived at the inspired life he's living today.

When John was a young boy, he was enthralled by baseball (and is to this day). "His" team is the St. Louis Cardinals and he grew up listening to the baseball games on the radio. As a result, he was very familiar with the famous voice of the sportscaster for the Cardinals, Jack Buck. John revered Jack.[152]

So just imagine young John lying on a hospital bed, strapped down, burned from head to toe, his eyes swollen shut, a ventilator in, experiencing searing pain, and not expected to survive the night. Imagine John hearing the voice of his hero Jack—not on the radio but at his bedside, not announcing the progress of a game but sharing words to give him a will to live. John said, "Jack Buck changed my life"[153] and he doesn't use those words lightly. His book unfolds just how profound Jack's presence and perspective were to young John, but it all began with their encounter in the hospital in 1987.[154]

Jack had not been a friend of the O'Leary's before the fire; he had not known the family before coming to the bedside of that burned little boy from St. Louis, Missouri. Jack Buck heard about John O'Leary from baseball great Red Schoendienst. Red heard about John from Red's daughter Colleen. Colleen heard about John from her neighbor. Her neighbor heard about John from a friend. That friend heard about John from another friend. And that other friend was a neighbor of the O'Leary's.[155]

We humans are profoundly connected and our decisions—even conversations—have a far-reaching effect. Thanks to a series of connections, Jack Buck's voice was the start of great things to come for John O'Leary. Jack, and many others, were pivotal players in John's road to recovery. In fact, John credits Jack for being his motivation to re-learn to write: John's fingers had to be amputated, they were so badly destroyed by the fire. But when John returned home with little stubs on his hands, it was Jack who mailed him autographed baseballs—one at a time, telling him he'd only get another if he wrote a thank you.

Jack Buck's voice was dominant in John's mind, but unfortunately his wasn't the only one John heard. When John's parents took him to a hand surgeon to see if he could make what was left of the deformed hands more functional, the doctor said, "If he was a horse, I'd shoot him."[156]

And right there is a stark lesson for all of us—by our choices and example, what "voice" do we want to be for others? The voice of hope that Jack Buck was? Or the voice of despair that the surgeon was? Both have the power of a ripple effect, but they are clearly not equal.

John's philosophy to "live inspired"[157] is the fruit of listening to the positive voices in his life, and through that, he pays it forward to others. And so, acknowledging that our words and actions have an impact on others, rather than embracing an example of despair and giving up on life that will inevitably spread to others, we ought to choose a life-affirming path that inspires others to join along.

10

Beauty and Creativity are Transformative

"A man should hear a little music, read a little poetry, and see a fine picture every day of his life, in order that worldly cares may not obliterate the sense of the beautiful which God has implanted in the human soul."
—Goethe[158]

I love that quote! Having played the piano for more than 30 years, I have experienced the soul-stirring, beautiful power of music and believe we should always have a daily dose. In fact, some of my best talks and writings have been composed as I listened to "epic music playlist" or "movie soundtrack playlist" on *YouTube*. As I write this, I am listening to some of the best scores of composer Hans Zimmer.

Music cannot be touched nor can it be seen. And yet, it is one of the most powerful invisible forces in our world.

I think it's safe to say my love of music began in the womb, since before I came along my mom had spent years as a performer, singing with her twin and a friend in a trio; that background has led her to always be humming something. With the passing of time, music became more and more a part of my life. I took singing lessons as a child and have my Grade 8 Certificate from *The Royal Conservatory of Music* for piano. But I would have to say my deepening love of music came out of the darkest period of my life.

When my engagement ended, my 35th birthday was only six weeks away. And the plan had been for my then-fiancé's family to celebrate with my family. With that plan no longer coming to fruition I needed to figure out an alternative so the day didn't feel entirely depressing.

As a social butterfly who firmly believes we are made for relationship and who agrees with Dostoyevsky that ***"beauty will save the world,"***[159] the new celebration developed: go to church, brunch with family which included holding close my sweet 2-year-old niece as I blew out my candles, dinner with friends, and finally, all of that concluding with one of my favorite activities: singing in the sunset amidst the beauty of one of Vancouver's beaches with the sounds of my friends' harmonizing voices. When I went to bed that night, my heart was full. And that's where the story begins.

But first, let's rewind a bit: Several years ago at a pro-life exhibit, I asked a depressed-looking university student, ***"What gives you joy? When are you fulfilled?"*** His answer, and our subsequent exchange, is for another day (and is discussed in my book *Love Unleashes Life: Abortion and the Art of Communicating Truth*). But in recalling that encounter, I realize my questions for him are also questions for me. And although I have many answers, my main ones are these: being in relationship with God, connecting with and helping others, immersing myself in music, and being surrounded by beauty.

That answer is what drew me to the activities I pieced together for my birthday. But who says those should only happen once per year? I thought to myself, "Is it possible that what makes me come alive makes others come alive too? Aren't we all made for relationship, and are there others in this technology-focused culture looking for opportunities for what we were made for: union and communion, i.e., human connection?" Time and again, my life has taught me to "lead, and others will follow." So after the success of "Singing in the Sunset" on my birthday, I confirmed with one of my friends that she would join me if I created a weekly summer gathering just like it. With a guarantee of one attendee, I then sent a message to a handful of friends asking if they would join for a weekly gathering beginning with going to church followed by migrating to the beach and singing while God paints us a sunset. Then I circulated it to an e-mail list. Then to a *Facebook* group.

And they came:

- From six people to over thirty people
- From those who were intending to come, to those we spontaneously invited because they happened to be at church beforehand
- From a 3-year-old old singing an old Australian song to a 75-year-old priest doing a jig and leading us in a rousing chorus of *Frere Jacques*
- From the stranger who joined us after his nearby game of volleyball, to the Chinese tourists walking past who, in broken English, requested we sing *Country Roads* because it was the only song they knew in English
- From starting out with one guitar, to a whole family of instruments making their way to our party: a mandolin, ukuleles, shakers, drums, a toy flute, and, going really exotic here—a digeridoo
- From praising God with *How Great Thou Art* to rocking it out to *The Lion Sleeps Tonight*

It. Was. Amazing.

I am quite confident that I would have organized none of this had I not found myself in a new situation that necessitated creating new experiences. Wedding planning is what I had in mind for that summer—not shattered dreams. But even from the most unexpected and painful of situations, God's grace can bring about new experiences of joy. When one chapter ends sadly, it doesn't mean there aren't other good—even great—chapters to be written.

The whole experience reminded me of this quote I once heard:

"Hope is like a bird that senses the dawn and carefully starts to sing

even while it is still dark." [160]

For those who feel surrounded by darkness, how we can we help them turn the light on? When someone feels that dying is better than living, what beauty can we introduce into their world?

Music is an invisible power that can turn light on in darkness and can bring beauty to a world of ugliness. Music stirs the heart; it lifts the spirits; it soothes the soul; it unlocks memories.

The documentary *Alive Inside* demonstrates this. It shares the story of a social worker who visits elderly people with dementia who live in care homes. He finds out what music individual patients listened to in their younger years and creates a personalized playlist. What he discovered was that people who had lost so much of their memories could nonetheless recall lyrics from decades prior. What he learned was that those who presented externally as being lifeless were actually "alive inside" when familiar songs were re-introduced to their world. By his example he teaches us that our gift to these individuals is not to lead them out of the world through assisted suicide, but rather to allow ourselves to be led into theirs. Music does that in a powerful way.

Dementia is one such condition where some people believe assisted suicide is the answer. "After all," they wonder, "Who would want to live in such a miserable state?" In response, I think of my friend Nicole Scheidl who created an organization called *Fit Minds* as a way of helping people with dementia. At fitminds.ca they write,

> Our vision is to give unprecedented support to seniors to be all they can be. We provide customized cognitive coaching to… build cognitive resilience. Our mission is to slow the advancement of dementia, improve the quality of life for seniors, create hope and meaningful relationships and use our business to bring joy to seniors.[161]

Fit Minds and *Alive Inside* are proof that we can alleviate suffering without eliminating people.

I saw the truth of this before my very eyes. As a result of a couple summers of "Sunset Singing" I was not content to sing only. But I also knew that bringing my piano to the beach was simply not a possibility. With several friends showing up with ukuleles I thought to myself, "Four strings? Super small?! I can learn that!" And so began my love-affair with the ukulele, an instrument I now play more than my piano. When I travel at airports with its case on my back, strangers will often approach and ask, "Is that a violin?" My favorite response is to say, "No—it's even better. It's a ukulele." That usually elicits a surprised look, to which I respond, "A violin is inherently sad. But the ukulele is like the accordion: it's an inherently happy instrument!"

As a result of learning the ukulele, it's not only a joy for me, but it has become a gift I give to others (including to my *Uber* drivers who have enjoyed my free "concerts"). I have had the opportunity to play and sing for all kinds of people, including a sick elderly woman who said, "When I hear the music my pain goes away."

On another occasion, I played for a woman with dementia and when I began with, "You are my…" she immediately chimed in "sunshine! My only sunshine…" She clearly hadn't forgotten everything.

I have seen music literally move people to tears. One particularly poignant encounter was with an older gentleman who requested the song my little nephew always asks me to play: Johnny Cash's *Ring of Fire*. Needless to say, I was happy to oblige. I got only two lines in when he began to weep. I slowed down and gently asked, "Do you want me to stop or do you want me to keep going?" I knew that music had power to flood the mind with memories and, even if these were painful, sometimes people want to "stay there" for a moment. They want to feel again. This man did; he told me to keep going.

When I eventually brought the song to its end, I looked at his tear-stained face and softly said, "Music can stir in our hearts deep emotions. I can see this song did that for you. Do you want to share about it?"

And so began an hour-plus conversation where he talked about broken relationships and painful regret, about walls built around the heart and the power of love to break them down, about connection, loss, contribution, and admiration; in short, we talked about his journey of life, and all the burdens he was still carrying in his heart. Music became the door to this expression, release, and processing.

Instead of assisting people with suicide, we should ask, "How can we assist them with processing their past and moving forward with hope?" And how can beauty be an instrument for accomplishing that?

We should work, for example, at making environments more esthetically pleasing; second-hand stores have a wide selection of canvas and other beautiful art that's economical and we could use for decorating places that people who are sick spend a lot of time in. Flowers always brighten a room, and carnations are an inexpensive kind that last a long time.

Or I think of what my cousin did to surround herself with beauty when she was very sick. Belinda, who I referenced in Chapter 3 (who surprised me by redecorating my basement suite), has faced many health challenges. The latest was December 2018, when she had major chest surgery as well as a hysterectomy (removal of the uterus, fallopian tubes, an ovary, and cervix). This was because she had endometriosis not only in her pelvis but also, incredibly, in her chest cavity. This debilitating and rare condition (called thoracic endometriosis) meant that when her uterus bled cyclically, so did cells inside her chest cavity. It resulted in ten episodes of a collapsed lung and four thoracic lung surgeries. All that unknowingly began when Belinda was seven weeks pregnant with her son and contracted H1N1, and had a three-liter fluid collection around her right lung. When her lung was drained, the needle punctured her diaphragm, creating a hole that was stretched by that pregnancy and the next, resulting in her liver herniating through her diaphragm into her thoracic (chest) cavity. This created an entrance for the endometriosis where cells from the uterus migrated through the diaphragm into her chest cavity. Before this was discovered, she was diagnosed with rheumatoid arthritis, which causes great pain in her wrists, hands, knees, toes and cervical spine. When the thoracic endometriosis was eventually discovered and she had all the surgeries, complications such as a bowel obstruction occurred after one surgery and pneumonia after another.

Needless to say, the past few years of her life involved much suffering and many hospitalizations. And yet, she was very intentional about beauty and creativity in an otherwise depressing time—she had her husband pack her cozy duvet from home to avoid the ugly, thin hospital blanket. When I would tuck her in at night, she had me spray lavender essential oil around her in order to mask the various hospital smells. She had a morning routine that helped her feel fresh and energized: A new set of pajamas for the day that were different from what she slept in, plus a morning routine of makeup application—"Look better, feel better" was her philosophy. Handmade pictures from her children decorated her room. She even brought a fine bone china teacup from home in order to drink tea from that instead of the hospital's blue plastic mug. These were a collection of little things but they made a big difference. And, of course, a continuous stream of family and friends helped move her painful days along.

Beauty. Creativity. These are what we should aspire towards, not assisted suicide.

When I think of the power of creativity as part of our response to the sick, I immediately think of Dr. Paul Brand. As a child of missionaries, he grew up in India. He moved to England to attend medical school and it was during WWII that he became a physician. He then returned to India to work as a doctor, specifically to serve people with leprosy (also called Hansen disease).

Dr. Brand came to realize that leprosy was a problem of nerves, not tissue—that the breakdown of fingers and toes, for example, was not because leprosy was "eating away" at them but because a leper's inability to feel pain caused him or her to unwittingly do self-destructive things. In his book, *The Gift of Pain: Why We Hurt & What We Can Do About It*, co-authored by Philip Yancey, he cites a case of a woman cooking a yam over a fire. When the yam accidentally fell off a stick, Dr. Brand, a hand surgeon, watched in horror as the woman called for a person nearby who had leprosy to reach his hand into the burning hot coals in order to retrieve the yam. Because he felt no pain he didn't think twice about subjecting his limb to such devastating destruction.[162]

Dr. Brand responded to the plight of leprosy patients by unleashing creativity—doing restorative hand surgeries and teaching them how to be consciously careful when doing activities, as well as how to check their bodies for signs of sores.

He learned to unleash even more creativity when some of his patients returned to him after he had restored their hands to an aesthetically pleasing and functional state. One patient said, "Dr. Brand, these are not good hands,"[163] a sentiment he was to discover other patients felt. The patient explained: His previously-crippled hands were an asset for when he begged. Now that his hands were repaired, he no longer succeeding in making enough money while begging to provide for his needs. But finding work was also not an option because leprosy had left his face with scars and markings that deterred people from employing him.

Dr. Brand reflected,

> My stomach twisted in a knot as John told me of the rejection he had encountered in the outside world. When he tried to board a public bus, sometimes the driver would physically throw him off. He, an educated man, was now unemployed and homeless, sleeping in an open plaza. He barely earned enough money from his begging to buy food. What had I done, repaired his body just enough to ruin his last chance for a livelihood?
>
> ***
>
> ...In order to equip leprosy patients for life on the 'outside,' we would have to change our approach radically. We must lift our sights from the narrow field of surgery on hands and feet and bring the whole person into view.[164]

Dr. Brand had the ears to hear what his patient was communicating but not verbalizing. When John said, "These are not good hands," what he was really expressing was this: *Fixing my hands has not entirely fixed my problem. Please help me.*

And so, rather than undo the surgery he had done, rather than maim patients so they could better beg, Dr. Brand got creative and did surgery to transfer hair from the scalp to above the eyes in order to re-grow eyebrows for leprosy patients who had lost theirs, and he also did plastic surgery to reconstruct the sunken noses many sufferers of the condition were marred with. By doing this, he removed the obvious signs of having had leprosy, and opened the door to new opportunities for his patients.

Dr. Brand's wife Margaret was equally creative. Also a physician, she worked in ophthalmology and was deeply troubled that a majority of leprosy patients experienced damage to their eyes (blindness was a troubling and frightening reality for many).

Have you ever had a staring contest with a friend and tried not to blink? Eventually both parties cave, often declaring as they fight back the urge to close their eyelids, "Ouch! That hurts." After a while, not blinking hurts. But what if you can't feel the hurt? Then you won't blink, as was the case for many leprosy patients who lost pain sensation in their eyes. But not blinking meant such a person's eyes would dry out and be more likely to develop damage and ulceration (again, just think about when you get something like a dust particle in your eye—it hurts so you blink and try to get it out, but people with leprosy won't feel that pain; with dust and other irritants not consciously aggravating them, the eye won't respond in a protective way).

Dr. Brand wrote of his wife, "Early on, Margaret saw a vivid illustration of the kind of abuse that can happen to a patient whose eyes are insensitive to pain: a man reached up and vigorously rubbed his open eyes with a hand covered with huge, crusty calluses. Little wonder her patients were going blind!"[165]

When Dr. Margaret failed at teaching her leprosy patients to consciously think of blinking, she came up with another solution; she implemented the surgical technique of Sir Harold Gillies: "It involved detaching one end of part of the temporalis muscle, which controls clenching of the jaw and chewing, and connecting it to a strand of fascia running through the eyelids."[166] And so, when her patients chewed gum, or food, their eyelids would blink, providing the much-needed lubrication for the surface of the eyes.

The Brand's creativity led to all kinds of fascinating things. For example, Dr. Paul added "cat breeder" to his resume in response to another problem he discovered: Some leprosy sufferers were coming to him and reporting that they were waking up with parts of their fingers or toes missing after sleeping. Dr. Brand was confused about how this would happen when the patient was at rest. One night, as a leprosy patient slept, a fellow patient sat watching. At one point he noticed a rat climb onto the bed and go up to the man's finger. Because he did not have sensation, he did not react and the rat began to chew the flesh of the patient—of course, the observer's screams intervened and put an end to the rodent's feast. But the mystery was identified. Dr. Brand's creative solution? Breed cats and send one home with each of his leprosy patients so they had a cat to sleep with, which would ward off rodents.[167]

The suffering of the Brand's patients was profound. But never was the Brand's solution to end their patients' lives. Instead, it was to get creative and find new, and out-of-the-box, ways to end their patients' suffering. Similarly, when someone says, "I want assisted suicide," the task of a truly caring individual is to hear what is being communicated but not verbalized, to search for what is underneath their request, and to get creative about a life-affirming response.

Moreover, there is a deeper message we can take away from the Brand's than just the power of creativity. Their work teaches us something we might initially recoil at: Pain matters. Pain is important. Pain is a ***gift***. Why? Because pain is a messenger. Certainly we shouldn't leave someone in a pain-riddled state (just think about the excruciating condition of EB mentioned in Chapter 4) but we should listen to it. Simply put, pain (whether physical, emotional, psychological, or spiritual) is telling us something is wrong. People with leprosy teach us that when we don't feel pain, all kinds of destructive things happen to us and hurt us more than pain itself. So when we do feel pain and anguish, it's an opportunity to ask, *What is this pain an indicator of? Is emotional pain a sign I have closed people out of my life? Is it a sign I have been traumatized in my past and yet to deal with something? Is physical pain a sign of cancer growing that, if not felt, would be a silent killer?* There are endless reasons for the various pains we may endure but when we feel pain, rather than run to assisted suicide, we should pause and explore what pain is telling us, and then respond with beauty and creativity.

This idea is captured in a poem composed almost 100 years ago by Myra Brooks Welch. She has the reader imagine an auction occurring, where an old violin is up for sale. The instrument is so battered and dusty that the auctioneer's attempts to entice a buyer prove futile. But then an old man steps forward. He wipes away the dust. He tunes the strings. And he plays a sweet melody.

After that, the auctioneer tries once more to sell the violin, and does so at an amount ***three thousand times*** the original asking price.

The awed audience wonders what made the difference. And someone cries out (as the poem is aptly titled), "The touch of the Master's hand."[168]

How often do people, like the patients of Drs. Brand or so many others, feel like the old violin? How often do sickness, disease, disability, and suffering make one feel like a worthless instrument to be rejected rather than prized? Assisted suicide feeds that false narrative. Instead, we are affirmed when we surrender ourselves "to the touch of the Master's hand" who uses creativity and beauty to "make all things new" (Revelation 21:5).

Epilogue

"Some people come into our lives and quickly go. Some stay for a while and leave footprints on our hearts and we are never, ever the same."[169]

My friend Alex is one such person who left footprints on my heart. Interestingly, my in-the-flesh encounters with him were few, but the impact was lasting. My first meeting was in 2013 during a family meal along with his wife Elaine, their young children Samuel and Esther (ages 4 and 2, respectively), and a couple of their friends. I had just made a short-term move to Eastern Canada and, knowing about my pro-life work, they had demonstrated their charism of hospitality and welcomed me to their home.

What struck me most that night was how gentle they all were. It was a beautiful demonstration of the passage from Colossians 3:15: "[L]et the peace of Christ control your hearts." There was a tangible and profound serenity radiating from each of them. It was remarkable and would be something I experienced in subsequent encounters.

Only a few months after that first meeting, Alex would be diagnosed with brain cancer. He was 34.

For the next five years, Alex was like a candle—he burned brightly. In between brain surgeries he even edited a major writing project for me, making significant improvements and helpful editorial contributions. And yet, as all wicks eventually dwindle, sadly Alex's time in this world would, too. Shortly before his 40th birthday, Alex's earthly pilgrimage came to an end.

I was part of a group of friends and family who regularly received e-mail updates from Alex over the years of his cancer journey. What always struck me was his disposition. Never was he angry at God. Instead, he lived day-by-day, praying he would live to see his children's children, believing God could heal him, and trusting—regardless of whether his prayers were answered as he wished—that God was good.

With Elaine's permission, I have included a few of Alex's messages sent in the final year and a half of his life. Alex's words are part of his rich legacy. They are a beacon for each of us, illuminating a perspective for how to live—and how to die. By his example, Alex taught me what I hope this book has taught you: to treasure the gift of life for as long as we are given it, to use our time to love and be loved, and to live in submission to our Heavenly Father whose ways are not ours.

July 24, 2017

Beloved,

Yesterday, marked the fourth year since God's right hand began specifically sustaining me under the prognosis of brain cancer. It was 4 years ago, yesterday, when I suffered a seizure in the parking lot of [a mall], leaving me unconscious. Samuel was 4 years old. Esther was 2. Both were strapped into their stroller that morning. Both were protected by the Lord through the first-responder on the scene, a police officer.

I was rushed to [the] hospital where a 5cm mass was found... I was transferred to [another hospital]. After undergoing brain surgery, I learned that the tumor was too invasive to remove. Second, I would come to learn that the tumor was malignant. Third, I would learn that God is faithful to supply what is needed for each day.

Four years ago, I did not anticipate that I would be writing this update. I did not anticipate that I'd have celebrated Samuel's 8th birthday with him. I did not anticipate that Elaine and I would be planning Esther's 6th birthday. Four years ago, I did not anticipate that Elaine and I would be preparing to celebrate our 11th wedding anniversary. Each of these milestones is an unspeakable manifestation of God's kindness to me.

So, on this day, I simply want to update you that my heart rejoices in God my Savior for He has done great and mighty deeds. Holy is His name!

I love Jesus today more than I ever have. He is my beloved and I am His. I know He loves me. Though medically my future may be uncertain, His love endures forever.

With love, Alex

September 20, 2017

Beloved, a couple of weeks ago, my pastor preached from Psalm 150. This Psalm is a psalm (song) of praise. Its final verse says, "Let everything that has breath praise the Lord" (Psalm 150:6). Since I have breath, I am included in this command. Regardless of my physical condition, allow me to praise the Lord.

1. I praise the Lord because He is the one who forgives all sins and heals all diseases (Psalm 103:3-4).

2. I praise the Lord for competent and

compassionate medical professionals who are using their education and experience to work for my health and my care.

3. I praise the Lord that though my Avastin treatments were extremely expensive, the Lord provided a grant to help offset some of the cost of the treatments. Without my knowledge, my medical team applied for this grant. I only found out after I had been selected to receive it.

4. I praise the Lord for my team of therapists at [the rehabilitation center] where I am receiving specialized physiotherapy and occupational therapy. I praise the Lord for these professionals who are patient with me as I relearn how to walk and how to write.

5. I praise the Lord for the freedom I have to grieve and feel sadness. Watching Samuel and Esther grow up and not being able to physically participate in all that they are involved does bring me sadness. Yet, I praise the Lord that he invites me to express that sorrow to him and I have often taken up that invitation.

6. I praise the Lord for Elaine who continues to maintain the home with grace and charity despite my limitations.

7. I praise the Lord for the body of Christ in different spheres of my life - who support me and stand with me in many practical ways: by praying for me and my family, driving me to appointments, mowing the lawn, preparing meals and sharing out of their abundance.

8. I praise the Lord for mornings spent with my children, reading the Bible and praying before they head off for school.

9. I praise the Lord for different family and friends who have moved into the house to help care for me for a season and to give Elaine a hand with day-to-day tasks.

10. I praise the Lord for my school community where Elaine and I teach and where Samuel and Esther study…and the love, care and support that it has offered me and my family during this season in our lives.

As I bring this update to a close, I invite you to join me in praising God for all his benefits. On Thursday, Sept. 21, I will have an MRI to see how the first two infusions of Avastin have worked. Please pray for a good report which will allow me to return to work as soon as possible.

Also pray for the restoration of my fine motor skills. I am having to relearn how to write. It is certainly humbling to be learning the same things as my 6 year old daughter!

Thank you for standing with me in prayer. I look forward to giving you a good report of answered prayer.

With sincere love, Alex

April 6, 2018

Beloved,

Grace and peace to you in Jesus Christ.

By God's grace, I was able to return to work on a part-time basis at the beginning of February, and have been blessed to be teaching and ministering… once again.

However, today we had some difficult news during an MRI follow up. I have been experiencing increased weakness and coldness in my left hand and foot. Doctors ruled out the possibility of blood clots, but seem to think that the tumor is now progressing. This is concerning, since we are presently using the last available treatment option.

While I will continue with my present treatment for now in order to slow down this progression, the doctors are suggesting that I focus on making the most of my time with my family, since the prognosis does not look promising.

Please continue to lift us up in prayer, that God would heal me, strengthen me and lengthen my life by decades so that I will see my children's children. Pray for our children and for God's wisdom for us to discern what to tell them and when.

Here is a reflection I wrote. Please pray that the remaining days/decades of my life would be invested in what is crucial, not what is trivial:

A matter or issue which is "crucial" is one which is extremely important. The root of "crucial" is "crucis"—the cross. I find it significant that in English, when a person wishes to indicate that something is extremely important, they have to refer to the cross. It was the apostle Paul, writing to Corinthian Christians who said,

> For I handed on to you as of first importance what I also received: that Christ died for our sins in accordance with the scriptures; that He was buried; that He was raised on the third day in accordance with

the scriptures; that He appeared to Kephas, then to the Twelve (1 Corinthians 15:3-5).

If "first importance" is synonymous with "crucial" then Paul is essentially saying that what is ultimately crucial is the "crucis," where Jesus died in the place of a sinner like me, His burial and His resurrection. This is what is "crucial."

Father in heaven, I ask that my life be invested in what is literally crucial—the death, burial and resurrection of your Son. In Jesus' name, Amen.

With love, Alex

June 19, 2018

Beloved in Christ,

Thank you for your ongoing support and your steadfast love shown to me and my family.

Since the end of April, I have been spending time at home with Elaine. We have also been keeping the children home two days a week, so that we can enjoy time as a family.

I am showing signs of increasing physical weakness and the most recent MRI revealed significant tumor growth. As a result, I have discontinued my treatments, but my faith in Jesus remains unshaken. We look to him each day as our joy and strength. Though my outward body is wasting away, my joy in Jesus Christ increases and the peace I know is beyond understanding.

I have been meditating on the Hebrews as they

left Egypt. From their perspective, with every step they took away from Egypt and towards the Red Sea, the Hebrews must have surmised that they were proceeding towards their ultimate demise, especially with the Egyptian army behind them. From God's perspective, God knew that with every step they took away from Egypt and towards the Red Sea, the Hebrews were proceeding towards their ultimate deliverance regardless of the Egyptian army behind them. In the same way, I know that with each passing day, I am moving closer to my ultimate deliverance and for this I am grateful.

We have had many visitors coming in and out of our house and I've had the opportunity to share with them the encouragement I find in Psalm 103. I regularly find myself reading and meditating on this Psalm…

Along with praying for me, I would covet your prayers for Elaine. She is carrying a heavy load emotionally and a heavy load physically. One year ago, there were two pairs of hands to maintain the home. Now it is Elaine who has to maintain the home largely on her own. She needs physical, emotional and spiritual strength for each new day.

Also, pray for Samuel and Esther, now nine and almost seven. They are fully aware of all that is transpiring and I desire that they will not grow bitter towards the Lord as they observe what is happening. Please pray that the outcome of this season in our lives will see them with gentle and tender hearts towards the Lord.

God bless, Alex

Start with What

September 10, 2018

Dear Friends and Family,

We are so grateful to God for all of you and the love and support you have shown us.

We wanted to update you on Alex's health, and to ask for your continued prayers for our family. Alex was recently admitted to [the] hospital… where a scan confirmed further swelling and probable tumor progression. The doctor put him onto a very high dose of steroids, which is intended to improve his symptoms for a period of time.

The steroids have improved these initial symptoms. However, Alex is weak and his mobility is very restricted... At this point we are remaining in the hospital, where we are receiving excellent care from a compassionate and competent medical team.

Please uphold Alex in your prayers. Pray that he would know God's healing power, and sense God's joy and peace daily. Pray that the children would have peace in a very difficult and busy time, as I am rushing between the hospital and home each day. Pray that God would grant me strength and peace also as I seek to bless and assist Alex at this time.

A verse I have found so much comfort in this summer comes from Isaiah 30:15... "In repentance and rest is your salvation, in quietness and trust is your strength."[170]

We seek to rest and trust in the goodness of God, and look to him as our strength and salvation.

Sending love to you all, Elaine and Alex, Samuel and Esther

November 4, 2018

Dearest Family and Friends,

Early this morning, around 4am, Alex passed peacefully into the arms of Jesus… We could not have asked for a more gracious closure to his life.

We are so thankful for each of your prayers, and for the encouragement and care you have provided for us on this journey. Praise God, that even in death, we have hope in Christ:

"Do not let your hearts be troubled. You have faith in God; have faith also in me. In my Father's house there are many dwelling places. If there were not, would I have told you that I am going to prepare a place for you?" (John 14:1,2).[171]

With much love, Elaine

If anyone had faith that he could be healed, Alex did. And yet, God didn't heal him—that is, on this side of Heaven. Alex never wavered in his love of the Lord even as his wish to live to see his children's children would not come to fruition—at least, as we comprehend it.

I wrote Elaine, now left widowed to single-parent their two young children. I asked her, "Alex had such faith that God would heal him. How have you worked through the reality that He didn't? What advice do you have for people who have the same hope and may experience the same disappointment? Did you ever get angry at God? Why or why not?"

In her beautifully tender way, Elaine wrote,

One of the marked challenges I faced along this journey was how to interact with the people who kept insisting that if we simply trusted in faith, then God would heal. Alex himself would often cling to Bible verses that spoke of God's healing. I had no doubt that God could heal, but came to see that our posture of prayer should be like that of the woman who simply reached out her hand and grabbed hold of Jesus' cloak, knowing that power rested in Him. We must similarly stretch out our hands in eager expectation, knowing God can do miracles, but also recognizing that this side of heaven, sickness and death often remain. Until we reach heaven, we cannot claim complete health. Scripture says too much about suffering to allow for that. So our task is to boldly ask and then to wait upon the God who may heal now and who may heal in the life to come.

I am grateful that long before this journey began I had wrestled through this question of suffering and had been led to some truths that have shaped the way I viewed God in the midst of our great loss. While Scripture does not give us all the answers about a particular trial we endure, we can remember that the bookends of Scripture are paradise. God created a perfect world without sin or sickness, and is creating a world in which those things will be eradicated forever. But that is not all! In the middle of the story, where we humans suffer and grieve, Jesus came and met us in his own broken body, suffering not only with us but for us. That he suffers with us gives comfort for the heartaches we face. That he suffers for us gives us hope for the life to come.[172]

I could have ended this book with an epic story of someone who suffered, prayed for healing, and experienced a miracle. And while such a narrative can serve a beautiful purpose to show what *is* possible, it can also leave those who don't experience such a "happily ever after" feeling disappointed and unable to relate—perhaps even feeling left out. Even those who do experience miracles will, in other ways, still suffer, for suffering is the universal human experience. Because of that, we need a universal human response.

Humans are designed for connection and love, but suicide assistance disconnects and robs us of the very lives through which we love. And so, an opportunity lies before we who read this, we who are each in the middle of our own unique stories. And that opportunity is to illuminate the brighter path that is the alternative to suicide assistance. That path entails the quiet strength of surrender, an emphasis on beauty and creativity, and a focus on loving relationships. At the heart of it all, is to *Start with What* and to seek, and find, meaning in any circumstance. When we do that, we will bring to life these words of Leon Bloy:

> **"*There are places in the heart that do not yet exist; suffering has to enter in for them to come to be.*"**[173]

About the Author

Stephanie Gray Connors is an author and international speaker who began presenting at the age of 18. She has given more than 1,000 pro-life presentations over two decades across North America as well as in Scotland, England, Ireland, Austria, Latvia, Guatemala, Mexico, and Costa Rica. She has spoken at many post-secondary institutions such as the University of California, Berkeley, Cornell University, and the University of Virginia School of Law. In 2017, Stephanie was a presenter for the series *Talks at Google*, lecturing at Google headquarters in California.

Stephanie's audiences are vast, including medical and law students, churches of various denominations, seminaries, high schools, and conferences. She has spoken at events for YWAM (Youth With A Mission), Alliance Defending Freedom, and Colson Center for Christian Worldview, to name a few.

Stephanie has formally debated abortion advocates such as Princeton philosophy professor Peter Singer as well as late-term abortionist Dr. Fraser Fellows. She has also debated Dr. Malcolm Potts, the first medical director for International Planned Parenthood Federation. In 2019, Stephanie participated in a historic eight-woman debate on abortion at *La Ciudad de las Ideas* (CDI), an event similar to *TED Talks*, which was held in Puebla, Mexico.

Stephanie is also author of *Love Unleashes Life: Abortion & the Art of

Communicating Truth. She holds a Bachelor of Arts in Political Science from UBC in Vancouver, and a Certification, *with Distinction*, in Health Care Ethics from the NCBC in Philadelphia.

Learn more at **www.loveunleasheslife.com**

Acknowledgments

Andy Steiger, Steve Kim, John Neufeld, Nicole Scheidl, Howard Bright, Veronica Hermary, Taylor Hyatt, Dad, and Mom: Thank you so much for the time you dedicated to reading and improving this manuscript with your helpful editorial contributions.

Lisa Rumpel: Your resilience inspires me. Thank you for your witness and for countless hours of your company in Vancouver's best coffee shops working on our writing projects together.

Julia Hanley: Thank you for your hard work on the cover design (and for taking care of my coffee machine)!

My family and friends who let me share their stories within: Thank you for letting your now-publicized witness touch others' hearts. I believe it will inspire readers to creativity, faith, and fortitude.

Endnotes

[1] Original lyrics by Bobby Boyd, Jeff Hanna, and Marc Hummon. "Bless the Broken Road." 1994. https://theboot.com/story-behind-the-song-bless-the-broken-road-rascal-flatts/ Accessed July 20, 2020. This song was made popular by Rascal Flatts in 2004.

[2] Ligertwood, Brooke. "New Wine." Hillsong Music Publishing, 2017. https://hillsong.com/lyrics/new-wine/ Accessed May 25, 2020.

[3] https://www.bbc.co.uk/news/world-us-canada-44416727 Accessed July 20, 2020.

[4] https://www.forbes.com/sites/robertglatter/2019/05/20/suicide-rates-sharply-increase-among-young-girls-study-finds/ Accessed July 20, 2020.

[5] BBC has a program called "Religions of the World" which provides animations outlining key stories of major world religions: https://www.bbc.co.uk/programmes/articles/1pYRg2f202rqWHrp3ywhTyX/religions-of-the-world Accessed July 20, 2020.

[6] "The North Wind & the Sun." *The Aesop for Children.* Library of Congress, http://read.gov/aesop/143.html Accessed September 2, 2020.

[7] Information about Matt is available here: https://www.matthampsonfoundation.org/about-us/matt-hampson/ Accessed July 20, 2020.

[8] Hampson, Matt. "#GETBUSY LIVING." *YouTube,* uploaded by TEDx Talks, 22 November 2016, https://www.youtube.com/watch?v=wWdwP31Uxg Accessed July 20, 2020. Note: Those words are also from the movie *The Shawshank Redemption.*

[9] Scripture texts are from The New American Bible, St. Joseph Edition, Catholic Book Publishing Company, New York.

[10] Laurance, Jeremy. "The case of Daniel James divided supporters of assisted suicide." *The Independent,* 27 May 2011, https://www.independent.co.uk/life-style/health-and-families/health-

news/agony-of-helping-a-son-to-kill-himself-2289710.html Accessed July 20, 2020.

[11] David, Anna. "Father tells how paralysed rugby son took poison in Swiss flat." *Evening Standard,* 10 December 2008, https://www.standard.co.uk/news/father-tells-how-paralysed-rugby-son-took-poison-in-swiss-flat-6905536.html Accessed July 20, 2020.

[12] It is worth pointing out something my friend Alex Schadenberg drew my attention to. Alex has spent two decades educating people on euthanasia through his organization Euthanasia Prevention Coalition, and through his blog he shared insight from Gordon Friesen who wrote, "[O]nly somewhat less than one percent of the victims of spinal chord injuries will despair, renounce, and end their lives during the first crucial five years of recovery (and after that time, their specific suicide rates become statistically identical to those of the general population)" (Source: *Who really wants to die? Part V: The absence of suicidal desire amongst the survivors of catastrophic injury*, https://alexschadenberg.blogspot.com/2020/09/normal-0-false-false-false-fr-ca-x-none.html, September 21, 2020). This is important to show that suicide is not the "normal" response to paralysis or disability in general. Obviously legalizing euthanasia/assisted suicide will change that statistic, but it is important we realize that it is not the condition itself that is the greatest threat to these individuals, but rather a societal concept of a "life unworthy of life" is the greatest enemy to these lives.

[13] A list of the effects of paralysis can be viewed at the website of Christopher & Dana Reeve Foundation: https://www.christopherreeve.org/living-with-paralysis/health/secondary-conditions Accessed May 25, 2020.

[14] Frankl, Viktor. "Finding meaning in difficult times (Interview with Dr. Viktor Frankl)." *YouTube,* uploaded by iakhan90, https://www.youtube.com/watch?v=LlC2OdnhIiQ Accessed July 20, 2020.

[15] This section draws from what I wrote in my blog, "Finding Meaning in Suffering," posted on 7 December 2016, https://loveunleasheslife.com/blog/2016/12/6/finding-meaning-in-suffering-by-stephanie-gray

[16] Frankl, Viktor. "Finding meaning in difficult times (Interview with Dr. Viktor Frankl)." *YouTube*, uploaded by iakhan90, https://www.youtube.com/watch?v=LlC2OdnhIiQ Accessed July 20, 2020.

[17] Ibid.

[18] Ibid.

[19] Simon Sinek has given one of the most popular TED Talks of all time (https://www.ted.com/playlists/171/the_most_popular_talks_of_all Accessed July 20, 2020), which is based on his book *Start With Why,* where he proposes the importance of knowing one's reasons, one's "why," in order to achieve great businesses, influence, and social change.

[20] Information about Patrick taken from an ESPN story about him in 2006 as shown on YouTube, uploaded by harvesct: https://www.youtube.com/watch?v=9xwCG0Ey2Mg Accessed July 20, 2020.
[21] Ibid.
[22] Their book is called *I am Potential: Eight Lessons on Living, Loving, and Reaching Your Dreams.*
[23] *Lord of the Rings: The Fellowship of the Ring.* Directed by Peter Jackson, New Line Cinema, 2001.
[24] Learn about Michael in his memoir below, his website michael-morton.com, and the documentary *An Unreal Dream: The Michael Morton Story*, 2013.
[25] These details learned from the previous endnote.
[26] Learn more about The Innocence Project on their website here: https://www.innocenceproject.org/ And learn about their role in Michael's case here: https://www.innocenceproject.org/cases/michael-morton/
[27] Morton, Michael. *Getting Life: An Innocent Man's 25-Year Journey from Prison to Peace, A Memoir.* New York, Simon & Schuster, 2014, p. 233.
[28] Read Lisa's writings here: https://resilientcatholic.home.blog/author/resilientlisa/
[29] Not their real names.
[30] Frankl, Viktor E. *Man's Search for Meaning.* Boston, Beacon Press, 1992, p. 115.
[31] Berthia, Kevin. "The Impact of Listening." *Youtube*, uploaded by TEDx Talks, 27 July 2015, https://www.youtube.com/watch?v=HB2_1A68YDU Accessed July 21, 2020.
[32] Briggs, Kevin. "The bridge between suicide and life." *Youtube,* uploaded by TED, 14 May 2014, https://www.youtube.com/watch?time_continue=574&v=7CIq4mtiamY Accessed July 21, 2020.
[33] Elliott, Josh K. "San Francisco's 'Golden Gate Guardian' prevented more than 200 suicides." *CTV News,* 26 March 2018, https://www.ctvnews.ca/health/san-francisco-s-golden-gate-guardian-prevented-more-than-200-suicides-1.3858896 Accessed July 21, 2020.
[34] Alleyne, Blaise and Van Maren, Jonathon. *A Guide to Discussing Assisted Suicide.* Toronto, Life Cycle Books, 2017, ebook version.
[35] Ibid.
[36] This section taken from a booklet I wrote for The Chilliwack Pro-Life Society, *An FAQ about Euthanasia and Assisted Suicide.*
[37] The Universal Declaration of Human Rights, Full Text, http://www.un.org/en/documents/udhr/index.shtml, Accessed July 31, 2015.
[38] This section is taken from my blog "The Second-Last Word," 23 October 2017, https://loveunleasheslife.com/blog/2017/10/23/the-second-last-word-by-stephanie-gray

³⁹ *The Story of Monica, a Hutu Survivor.* International Alert, https://www.international-alert.org/stories/story-monica-hutu-survivor Accessed July 21, 2020.

⁴⁰ Bradley, Susan. "Penny Boudreau, who killed her daughter, to get escorted leaves from prison." *CBC News,* 5 July 2018, https://www.cbc.ca/news/canada/nova-scotia/penny-boudreau-murder-daughter-escorted-leaves-prison-1.4735247 Accessed July 21, 2020.

⁴¹ Favaro, Avis and St. Philip, Elizabeth. "This woman with an incurable disorder wants to end her life, but can't get assisted death." *CTV News.* 8 December 2019, https://www.ctvnews.ca/health/this-woman-with-an-incurable-disorder-wants-to-end-her-life-but-can-t-get-assisted-death-1.4720730 Accessed May 26, 2020

⁴² Points in this section taken from my blog "Assisted Suicide in Select Cases?" 8 May 2017, https://loveunleasheslife.com/blog/2017/5/8/assisted-suicide-in-select-cases-by-stephanie-gray

⁴³ Ibid.

⁴⁴ Eckholm, Eric. "Pfizer Blocks the Use of Its Drugs in Executions." *The New York Times,* 13 May 2016, https://www.nytimes.com/2016/05/14/us/pfizer-execution-drugs-lethal-injection.html?_r=1 Accessed July 21, 2020.

⁴⁵ "NEW VOICES: American Medical Association, EMT Association Say Participation in Executions Violates Medical Ethics." *Death Penalty Information Center,* 18 July 2006, https://deathpenaltyinfo.org/node/1775 Accessed July 21, 2020.

⁴⁶ Taken from my blog "Assisted Suicide in Select Cases?" 8 May 2017, https://loveunleasheslife.com/blog/2017/5/8/assisted-suicide-in-select-cases-by-stephanie-gray

⁴⁷ Briggs, Kevin. *Guardian of the Golden Gate: Protecting the Line Between Hope and Despair.* Kansas, Ascend Books, 2015, p. 113.

⁴⁸ Ibid., p. 281.

⁴⁹ This next section draws on my blog, "The Day I was Stumped." 30 March 2016, https://loveunleasheslife.com/blog/2016/3/30/the-day-i-was-stumped-by-stephanie-gray

⁵⁰ Frankl, Viktor Emil. *Man's Search for Meaning.* United Kingdom, Pocket Books, 1985, p. 57, online at Google Books, https://www.google.com/books/edition/Man_s_Search_For_Meaning/W3q8R4dRZTwC?hl=en&gbpv=0 Accessed September 2, 2020.

⁵¹ Briggs, Kevin, p. 273.

⁵² Ibid.

⁵³ Not their real name.

⁵⁴ Not her real name.

⁵⁵ Philosopher Peter Kreeft has written extensively on the topic of the existence of God. Learn more here: https://www.peterkreeft.com/

[56] "Heartsong" is a word used by Mattie Stepanek, an inspiring young boy whose story is told in a later chapter.

[57] Story, Laura. *When God Doesn't Fix It: Lessons You Never Wanted to Learn, Truths You Can't Live Without*. Tennessee, W Publishing Group, 2015, p. 224, 226, 236.

[58] "Laura Story." *CBN 700 Club.* https://www1.cbn.com/700club/laura-story Accessed July 21, 2020.

[59] Supreme Pontiff John Paul II. *Salvifici Doloris.* 1984, http://www.vatican.va/content/john-paul-ii/en/apost_letters/1984/documents/hf_jp-ii_apl_11021984_salvifici-doloris.html Accessed July 21, 2020.

[60] Learn about the Hoyt's here: http://www.teamhoyt.com/About-Team-Hoyt.html

[61] "Dick & Rick Hoyt." *YouTube*, uploaded by IRONMAN Triathlon, 5 February 2007, https://www.youtube.com/watch?v=dDnrLv6z-mM Accessed July 21, 2020.

[62] "The Story of Team Hoyt @ ESPY's 2013 – Jimmy V Perseverance Award." *Youtube*, uploaded by Keith Bergh, 19 July 2013, https://www.youtube.com/watch?v=xBXy1EH4nYc Accessed July 21, 2020.

[63] Ibid.

[64] Learn about their story here https://www.pushinc.us/about

[65] "I'll Push You: Embracing God's Promise of Provision." *Youtube*, uploaded by I'll Push You, 15 March 2016, https://www.youtube.com/watch?v=NfQpfi8qsR0&t=3030s Accessed July 22, 2020.

[66] Ibid.

[67] Ibid.

[68] Anderson Cooper 360°. *Twitter,* 15 August 2019, 10:05pm, video clip of CNN interview, https://twitter.com/AC360/status/1162183695270387712 Accessed July 22, 2020.

[69] This section is taken from a blog I wrote, "Comfortable in His Skin," https://loveunleasheslife.com/blog/2017/2/3/comfortable-in-his-skin-by-stephanie-gray

[70] Learn more about Moe here: https://vimeo.com/86757114

[71] Learn about Jonathan here: http://www.ctvnews.ca/health/butterfly-boy-jonathan-pitre-recovering-after-stem-cell-treatment-1.3065188

[72] Learn more about EB here: http://www.debra.org/ That quote is used under the section "About EB."

[73] "Euthanasia in Canada? The Coming World of Assisted Dying." *Youtube,* uploaded by Advokate Life & Education Services, 4 March 2015, https://www.youtube.com/watch?v=SCKVqnO4n2U Accessed August 7, 2015.

[74] This section taken from a booklet I wrote for The Chilliwack Pro-Life Society, *An FAQ about Euthanasia and Assisted Suicide*, also available here: https://loveunleasheslife.com/s/Euthanasia-FAQ.pdf

[75] "WHO Definition of Palliative Care." https://www.who.int/cancer/palliative/definition/en/ Accessed July 22, 2020.

[76] "How Will You Say Goodbye to Someone You Love?" Paper by the Euthanasia Prevention Coalition, January 2006.

[77] Bright, Julia. "Live Every Stage Fully." *Blog,* 22 November 2016. https://loveunleasheslife.com/blog/2016/11/22/live-every-stage-fully-by-dr-julia-bright

[78] Letter to Stephanie from Elaine.

[79] "What Really Matters at the End of Life." *Youtube,* uploaded by TED, 30 September 2015, https://www.youtube.com/watch?v=apbSsILLh28&t=80s Accessed July 22, 2020.

[80] Ibid.

[81] Bright, Julia. "Live Every Stage Fully."

[82] Dowdell, Andrew and Schneider, Kate. "Barry Sim and his wife Izzy Sim missed flight Malaysia Airlines flight MH17." *News.com.au*, 18 July 2014, https://www.news.com.au/travel/travel-updates/incidents/barry-sim-and-his-wife-izzy-sim-missed-flight-malaysia-airlines-flight-mh17/news-story/c64eb963a55ae6c11ed63c91dbc04d38 Accessed July 22, 2020.

[83] Pacholczyk, Tad. "Going Too Far with DNR?" *Making Sense of Bioethics,* April 2013, https://www.fathertad.com/files/9414/6917/1584/MSOB094_Going_Too_Far_with_DNR.pdf Accessed July 22, 2020.

[84] "Q&A from the USCCB Committee on Doctrine and Committee on Pro-Life Activities regarding The Holy See's Responses on Nutrition and Hydration for Patients in a 'Vegetative State.'" *United States Conference of Catholic Bishops,* http://www.usccb.org/_cs_upload/7666_1.pdf Accessed August 7, 2015.

[85] Pacholczyk, Tad. "Are Feeding Tubes Required?" *Making Sense of Bioethics,* December 2006, https://www.fathertad.com/files/8014/7025/5378/MSOB_018_Are_Feeding_Tubes_Required.pdf Accessed July 22, 2020.

[86] Learn more at https://terrischiavo.org/

[87] Timeline, https://terrischiavo.org/story/timeline/ Accessed July 22, 2020.

[88] Ibid.

[89] Ibid.

[90] *Principles of Medical Ethics,* MODULE 2-2 Readings, National Catholic Bioethics Center, National Certification Program in Health Care Ethics (course handout from 2008-09 year).

[91] "About Calvary Hospital." https://www.calvaryhospital.org/ Accessed September 20, 2020.

[92] "Meet Our Team." https://www.calvaryhospital.org/about/meet-our-team/michael-j-brescia-md/ Accessed September 20, 2020.

[93] "Dr. Brescia: An Interview with Sr. Mary Margaret Hope, SV." *Imprint.* Spring 2017 Issue, https://sistersoflife.org/wp-content/uploads/2019/05/SV-Imprint-Spring-2017.pdf Accessed September 2, 2020.

[94] Ibid.

[95] Ibid.

[96] *Mother Teresa: A Simple Path.* Compiled by Lucinda Vardey. New York, Ballantine Books, 1995, p. 79.

[97] Taken from my blog "An Encounter with Grace," https://loveunleasheslife.com/blog/2017/4/12/an-encounter-with-grace-by-stephanie-gra

[98] "Death with Dignity." *Youtube,* uploaded by Christopher Stefanick, 6 January 2015, https://www.youtube.com/watch?t=66&v=0nf_rb2qkbE Accessed July 22, 2020.

[99] "Dignity." *Merriam-Webster Dictionary Online,* https://www.merriam-webster.com/dictionary/dignity Accessed July 22, 2020.

[100] Watson, Leon. "Inside the Paris apartment untouched for 70 years: Treasure trove finally revealed after owner locked up and fled at outbreak of WWII." *Dailymail.com,* 12 May 2013, https://www.dailymail.co.uk/news/article-2323297/Inside-Paris-apartment-untouched-70-years-Treasure-trove-finally-revealed-owner-locked-fled-outbreak-WWII.html Accessed July 22, 2020.

[101] Ibid.

[102] Pistorius, Martin. *Ghost Boy: The Miraculous Escape of a Misdiagnosed Boy Trapped Inside His Own Body.* Tennessee, Nelson Books, 2013, p. 21, 55.

[103] Learn more about Martin here http://www.martinpistorius.com/tmpsite/#home and here https://twitter.com/martinpistorius?lang=en

[104] Pistorius, Martin, p. 182.

[105] These details are outlined in Henry's memoir, sourced below.

[106] Ibid.

[107] Fraser, Henry. *The Little Big Things: A Young Man's Belief that Every Day Can be a Good Day.* Great Britain, Seven Dials, 2017, p. 15.

[108] Ibid., p. 20.

[109] Ibid., p. 27.

[110] This section is drawn from my blog "The Secondary Emotion of Anger" here https://loveunleasheslife.com/blog/2019/2/18/the-secondary-emotion-of-anger-by-stephanie-gray

[111] *Walk the Line.* Directed by James Mangold, performances by Joaquin Phoenix, Reese Witherspoon, and Ginnifer Goodwin, Fox 2000 Pictures, 2005.

[112] Berger, Warren. *A More Beautiful Question: The Power of Inquiry to Spark Breakthrough Ideas.* New York, Bloomsbury, 2014, p. 191.

[113] Heller, Rachel and Levine, Amir. *Attached. The New Science of Adult Attachment and How it Can Help You Find—and Keep—Love.* New York, Penguin, 2011. p. 110.

[114] Campbell, Meagan. "Canada's Loneliest People." *Macleans*, 22 June 2018, https://www.macleans.ca/society/canadas-loneliest-people/ Accessed July 24, 2020.

[115] Ibid.

[116] "This Old Man is Healthy But Wants to Kill Himself." *YouTube.* Uploaded by ABC News In-depth, 18 July 2018, https://www.youtube.com/watch?v=tWDnW17-gNk Accessed July 24, 2020.

[117] Ibid.

[118] Gartry, Laura. "David Goodall: Australia's oldest working scientist fights to stay at university." *ABC News,* 26 August 2016, https://www.abc.net.au/news/2016-08-27/david-goodall:-australias-oldest-working-scientist/7788844 Accessed July 24, 2020.

[119] Hamlyn, Charlotte. "The final move." *ABC News,* 2 May 2018, https://www.abc.net.au/news/2018-05-05/david-goodall-trip-to-switzerland-for-voluntary-euthanasia/9716354 Accessed July 24, 2020.

[120] McKenzie, Sheena, Bell, Melissa, Vandoorne, Saskya, Westcott, Ben. "104-year-old scientist David Goodall 'welcomes death' at Swiss clinic." *CNN,* 9 May 2018, https://www.cnn.com/2018/05/08/health/david-goodall-australia-switzerland-interview-intl/index.html Accessed July 24, 2020.

[121] Bever, Lindsey. "David Goodall, 104, just took his own life, after making a powerful statement about assisted death." *The Washington Post,* 10 May 2018, https://www.washingtonpost.com/news/to-your-health/wp/2018/05/09/this-104-year-old-plans-to-die-tomorrow-and-hopes-to-change-views-on-assisted-suicide/ Accessed July 24, 2020.

[122] "This Old Man is Healthy But Wants to Kill Himself."

[123] Ibid.

[124] "What happens when a nursing home and a day care center share a roof?" *PBS News Hour,* 10 May 2016, https://www.pbs.org/newshour/show/what-happens-when-a-nursing-home-and-a-day-care-center-share-a-roof Accessed July 24, 2020.

[125] This and the next story are taken from my blog "A Resolution for the New Year: In the Face of Suffering, Unleash Love," https://loveunleasheslife.com/blog/2017/1/3/a-resolution-for-the-new-year-in-the-face-of-someones-suffering-unleash-your-love-by-stephanie-gray

[126] This section taken from my blog "The Circle of Life," https://loveunleasheslife.com/blog/2016/12/5/the-circle-of-life-by-stephanie-gray

¹²⁷ Sarah, Robert Cardinal. *The Power of Silence: Against the Dictatorship of Noise.* San Francisco, Ignatius Press, 2017, pp. 54, 69.

¹²⁸ "Brittany Maynard's Husband Tells Megyn Kelly About Her Decision To Die | Megyn Kelly TODAY." *YouTube,* uploaded by TODAY, 1 June 2018, https://www.youtube.com/watch?v=itihpltdVec Accessed July 25, 2020.

¹²⁹ Ibid.

¹³⁰ Ibid.

¹³¹ "Mattie Stepanek on Larry King Live." *YouTube,* uploaded by ProMedia, 7 July 2014, https://www.youtube.com/watch?v=D3ALna5Kg_M&t=583s Accessed July 25, 2020.

¹³² See link above.

¹³³ "World Over - Jeni Stepanek on Mattie Stepanek's Cause for Sainthood with Raymond Arroyo." *Youtube,* uploaded by EWTN, 20 July 2018, https://www.youtube.com/watch?v=DBUNIvbtkkI Accessed July 25, 2020.

¹³⁴ Ibid.

¹³⁵ Ibid.

¹³⁶ "About Mattie," http://mattiematters.org/about-mattie/ Accessed July 25, 2020.

¹³⁷ "#24: Meeting Mattie Stepanek | TV Guide's Top 25 | Oprah Winfrey Network." *Youtube,* uploaded by OWN, 29 August 2012, https://www.youtube.com/watch?v=3masTPPXfIU Accessed July 25, 2020.

¹³⁸ "How Mattie Stepanek's Words Inspired Millions | The Oprah Winfrey Show | Oprah Winfrey Network." *Youtube,* uploaded by OWN, 22 June 2014, https://www.youtube.com/watch?v=ZxD-U1rY0vw Accessed July 25, 2020.

¹³⁹ "World Over - Jeni Stepanek and Dr. Denise Hunnell with Raymond Arroyo - 09-01-2011 ." *YouTube,* https://www.youtube.com/watch?v=1EeR4DPr9LQ&t=926s Accessed July 25, 2020.

¹⁴⁰ Ibid.

¹⁴¹ O'Leary, John. "The Best Flight I Ever Missed." *John O'Leary Live Inspired,* 24 February 2020, http://johnolearyinspires.com/2020/02/the-best-flight-i-ever-missed/?mc_cid=b64bb30dc7&mc_eid=95492dac89 Accessed July 25, 2020.

¹⁴² Kubler-Ross, Elisabeth and Kessler, David. *Life Lessons: Two Experts on Death and Dying Teach Us About the Mysteries of Life and Living.* New York, Scribner, 2000, pp. 186-187.

¹⁴³ King, Martin Luther. "Letter from a Birmingham Jail." 16 April 1963, https://www.africa.upenn.edu/Articles_Gen/Letter_Birmingham.html Accessed December 3, 2020.

¹⁴⁴ This section is drawn from my blog "The Impact of Choices" here https://loveunleasheslife.com/blog/2017/1/12/the-impact-of-choices-by-stephanie-gray

¹⁴⁵ Chen, Tina. "Starbucks Customers Break 1,000 in Pay-It-Forward Record." ABC News, 27 December 2013, https://abcnews.go.com/blogs/headlines/2013/12/starbucks-customers-break-1000-in-pay-it-forward-record/ Accessed August 27, 2020.

¹⁴⁶ Dunn, James. "Woman born with no arms or legs reveals her empowering fight against bullies, abusers and suicidal thoughts to become an inspiration to thousands in Colombia." Mail Online, 28 July 2015, https://www.dailymail.co.uk/news/article-3177324/Woman-born-no-arms-legs-reveals-empowering-fight-against-bullies-abusers-suicidal-thoughts-inspiration-thousands-Colombia.html Accessed August 27, 2020.

¹⁴⁷ Ibid.

¹⁴⁸ Dow, David. "Lessons from Death Row Inmates." TEDxAustin, February 2012, https://www.ted.com/talks/david_r_dow_lessons_from_death_row_inmates?language=en Accessed August 27, 2020.

¹⁴⁹ Ellis Nutt, Amy. "Robin Williams' suicide was followed by a sharp rise in 'copycat' deaths." Chicago Tribune, 8 February 2018, https://www.chicagotribune.com/lifestyles/health/ct-robin-williams-suicide-copycats-20180208-story.html Accessed August 28, 2020.

¹⁵⁰ Ibid.

¹⁵¹ *National Suicide Prevention Strategies: Progress, Examples, Indicators.* Geneva: World Health Organization. 2018, https://www.who.int/mental_health/suicide-prevention/national_strategies_2019/en/ p. 9, Accessed August 28, 2020.

¹⁵² These details are outlined in John's book below.

¹⁵³ O'Leary, John. *On Fire: The 7 Choices to Ignite a Radically Inspired Life.* New York, Gallery Books, 2016, p. 166.

¹⁵⁴ The details of John's story are outlined in his book above.

¹⁵⁵ Ibid., pp. 170-171.

¹⁵⁶ O'Leary, John. "Saved from the Fire." Beliefnet, https://www.beliefnet.com/inspiration/articles/john-oleary-saved-from-the-fire.aspx Accessed August 28, 2020.

¹⁵⁷ Learn more at John's website https://johnolearyinspires.com/

¹⁵⁸ *Musical Mosaics: A Collection of Six Hundred Selections from Musical Literature, Ancient and Modern. Including Extracts from Many Later Critical and Asthetical Writings.* United States, T. Presser, 1889, p. 95.

¹⁵⁹ Dostoyevsky, Fyodor. *The Idiot.* Part III, chapter 5.

¹⁶⁰ This quote is throughout the internet and has been attributed as "unknown" or "anonymous," but a similar version of it is said by Rabindranath Tagore in the book *Fireflies* as, "Faith is the bird that feels the light and sings when the dawn is still dark."

¹⁶¹ "About Us." Fit Minds, https://fitminds.ca/vision-mission/ Accessed August 28, 2020.

[162] Brand, Paul and Yancey, Philip. *The Gift of Pain: Why We Hurt & What We Can Do About It.* Michigan, Zondervan, 1997, p. 6.

[163] Ibid., p. 135.

[164] Ibid. pp. 135-137.

[165] Ibid., p. 146.

[166] Ibid.

[167] Ibid., pp. 127-128.

[168] Welch, Myra Brooks. *The Touch of the Master's Hand.* All Poetry. 1921, https://allpoetry.com/Myra-Brooks-Welch Accessed August 28, 2020.

[169] Markham, Shelly, et al. Flavia and the Dream Maker: The Musical. United States, Dramatic Pub., 2004. p. 23

[170] This passage is from the New International Version (NIV) of the Bible.

[171] The version of the Bible used for this quote is different from the version Elaine used in order to be consistent with the rest of the Bible passages in this book.

[172] Letter from Elaine to Stephanie.

[173] Quoted in a book by Small, Phil. *On the Way to Here: Reflections on Things that Matter.* Australia, Friesen Press, 2017, p. 115.

Made in the USA
Monee, IL
31 January 2022